NO MORE AGAIN FOREVER

NO MORE AGAIN FOREVER

*The Pain You See Today,
You Will See No More
Again Forever*

DR. PATRICIA LOTT

Dominion Global Enterprises Publishing

Regardless of the season
don't you dare give up because
Dad has the most amazing plan
for you!

　　　Manifold Blessings
　　　Mrs. Patricia Lott

Contents

Photo Insert   iv

INTRODUCTION   I

    1   GOD WANTS TO MAKE A PERSONAL COVENANT
WITH YOU   4

    2   DON'T BURY ME UNTIL I AM DEAD!   14

    3   IS THERE RED IN YOUR LEDGER   21

    4   KINGDOM CONVERSATIONS   31

INTERLUDE   40

    5   WHEN YOU SAY YES TO THE LORD... BE
PREPARED   45

INTERLUDE   74

    6   TREATMENT WAS EASY... RECOVERY ALMOST
KILLED ME   79

    7   YOU CAN DO IT   102

EPILOGUE   107

ABOUT THE AUTHOR   112
MY SUPPORT TEAM (DOMINO'S)   113

INTRODUCTION

It was like one of those scenes in the movies when there was a loud, heavy silence, and everything was moving in slow motion. "Both of the places that we biopsied came back positive for cancer." Was this really happening to me or was it some kind of cruel dream I couldn't seem to wake myself up from? The ink pen that was in my hand dropped to the floor. My oldest Son Wayne picked it up and began asking the bearer of this news questions as she explained what this meant and what the next step would be. I felt the hand of my husband Wayne Sr. drop from my shoulder and rest on the small of my back. Was I passing out? I heard him say, Patti, it's going to be alright. Wait, that wasn't my guy because there was the sound of tears in his voice. Was this happening to me?

Seeing Guinevere Fuller's mouth moving, I see Wayne's (Jr's) handwriting; I feel my husband's hand squeezing mine, but I can't hear anything but silence. "Lord," I said, "Do you have a word of comfort for me?" I know that seems like a funny reaction to this news, however, at that moment, He was all that I could tap into. I couldn't connect with what was happening. I couldn't move. I desired to talk to my Heavenly Father, the one that I dedicated my life, faith, and trust to. I needed my Savior. Whatever the Lord's answer to me was, it would be sufficient. I have known for some time that He has a plan for me, and He Did! He answered me in the moment's stillness. The Lord whispered in my spirit, "The Egyptian that You See Today, You Will See No More Again Forever," and so began my journey with Breast Cancer.

I need to pause right here and speak to you, the one reading this book, and let you know that there is so much more in this book than just breast cancer and Patricia-Eileen. The lessons learned, the experiences shared, the hope conferred, and the fire spread are for You yes You and cancer has nothing to do with it. (That would be a statement that the Holy Spirit would whisper to me often on this journey and I wanted to share with you).

Along this journey that we call life, there are moments when there is no explanation for the information that we just heard or reasoning for the turn that life has taken us on. But one thing is for certain, it is a defining moment in the remaining of our existence. For me it was hearing the words, "The tests came back positive for cancer in two places in your breast." For you it may be the words, "I no longer desire to be married to you, I am filing or have filed for a divorce", It may be "After these years at this company I have to let you go", It could be "You will never walk again", or "Your child has died" It could be anything that you never imagined in all of your years that you would ever hear spoken to you. It is news that shakes you to your core and challenges how you perceive your existence and calls on you to decide whether to fight or fall. This book is for you.

It is the domino effect that happens when hearing this type of news. It now touches everyone with whom you are in contact with or that is in your bubble. In my case, it was my husband and my son who heard the Doctor's report with me. It was my husband who sat with me, making sure that I didn't drift away and get lost within myself. Wayne (Jr), my oldest son, contacted his siblings and my brother to let them know about this new direction that our family bubble was getting ready to take. It was these 7 people who were close to me whom I spoke many words of life too, who also referred to me as the strong one. They were now speaking life to me.

The doctor called it "A little hiccup" but it was a tsunami as the waves hit the family and friends. The same is true for you. Whatever the situation that your loved one found themselves in, you are now with them and on the sidelines at the same time. Your life has been touched merely because their life has touched you. You have been called to walk through this with them, yet you do not know what that looks like, what it entails, how to be of support, how to carry on with life, how to hold it together and move forward. This book is for you as well.

It is my prayer that as we walk through this journey together; you find things are not always as they seem... that in the middle of this there is an assignment for your life... through this you are being transformed more into the image of the Son and that because of your victory the body of Christ is edified, and the Lord has been glorified.

I

GOD WANTS TO MAKE A PERSONAL COVENANT WITH YOU

Genesis chapter 15 verse 18, "... In the same day, the Lord made a covenant with Abram..." You have to read the entirety from verse 1 to feel the weight of that statement. If you want to dig in, make a study of chapters 12-17. This would be the beginning of an understanding that this thing called cancer had less to do with a diagnosis than it had to do with learning to live by the word in all aspects of life. I know it feels like I dropped you in the middle of a thought, so let me back up, catch you up, and then move on.

It was December eighth. Exactly one week after having heard that, I had two forms of cancers in my body. I was sitting in a boardroom with a surgeon, a radiology oncologist, a medical oncologist, my doctor, my husband, my two sons, and on the speaker phone were my daughter and brother. We were discussing the journey that I was about to take. All the things that could go wrong, like loss of my hair, pain, burning, and nausea. They were also talking about the loss of my lymph nodes that would determine the stage of the cancer, etc., and to be honest, it got too big for me. I felt overwhelmed, feeling the tears wailing up as my son Michael (the one who is very few on words, who only talks when necessary) says, "Hold on. I need you to explain to me what you mean by 'aggressive' you have said that twice now, that one of these cancers is aggressive. What does that mean?" It was as if it sucked the air out of the room and the silence was deafening as we all waited to hear the answer that none of us had the courage to ask. "Well, it means that it is a fast-moving cancer that will more than likely result in death in 3-6 months if we don't deal with it right now." Boom! They pulled the rug out from under me. "What was going on?"

I remember saying, "Let's schedule the surgery for tomorrow" The specialist replied to me, "We want you to enjoy Christmas with your family. Let's schedule it for December 29th." Now what the enemy whispered to me was, "We want you to enjoy this last Christmas with your family because this cancer is going to kill you. This is how you leave here" So there I was again talking to my Daddy God. I couldn't wait to get to our prayer meeting or either my prayer closet to cry out to Him. I needed God NOW! I froze in my chair and to be honest, from a psychologist position (Physician, heal thyself right) I would have said that I dissociated. When in all actuality I was trying to figure out the quickest way to run out of that room down to the hospital chapel to pray.

Here's what happened. The Lord called me to Him and shook me out of that state and said these words to me: First, no one has the authority to put an expiration stamp on your life. I determine life and death. The second thing that he said to me was "If you won't accept any other spirit from the devil why are you accepting fear." Slam on the breaks and let's revisit that. OK! Not now, but a little later in this chapter, we will go deeper.

Then the Lord says to me, "Patti, if you will hearken diligently to do the things that I say unto you, if you do not stop preaching, do not stop praying and do not stop praising, I WILL NOT ALLOW THE SIDE-EFFECTS OF THIS TREATMENT TO COME UPON YOU for I am the Lord Your God and I am with you." Holy Moly! Did you just catch that? The Lord made a covenant with me concerning the journey that I was just about to take, and the Lord wants to make a covenant with you.

No one has the authority to put an expiration stamp on your life. I determine life and death.

So, you just received this devastating news and just when you thought things couldn't get any worse... they do. I get it and completely understand. Let me speak into your life man, woman, teen, and child, that when you are in a right relationship with the Lord, He has some-thing to say about your well-being if you will... listen and hear Him. I need to speak this into your spirit right now. No one has the power or authority to dictate when your life ends. No one! God reserves that power for himself. The enemy is banking on you getting caught up in the soulish or emotional realm so that you receive the word of man over the word of the Lord. He knows that if he can cause you to get so scared that you walk in fear and doubt, the enemy can come to kill, steal, and destroy. The devil knows if he can get you to prophesy or speak of your own failure or death, then he has won the battle.

I know the doctor has knowledge because of what the Lord has given to him. I know your spouse said they are leaving, or they reduced or took away your income. At the end of the day, who do you Trust? The Lord declared in his word that we are to take no thought what we are to eat, wear and live for our heavenly Father already knows what we have need of, so seek Him first.... Seek HIM FIRST and His righteousness and ALL of these things will be added unto you. It doesn't matter what anybody says. It matters what you believe about what God has said concerning you. You must train your ear to press close to the mouth of God, He has something to say to you that no one will understand or come into agreement with because it is for you, and it is concerning whatever you face at this length of your journey.

There are many voices out there, especially in the time in which we live, but I encourage you today whatever has just come to shake you to your core.... Understand that God has the final say about it. This is not the time to ask everyone their opinion. No one has been on this journey; it is your journey. Yes, there have been others diagnosed with cancer, but that was their journey, not mine. What God spoke concerning it was for me. They could not speak to me what the Lord wanted to speak to me. They could not bring any manifestation into my life. That was something that could only come from the Lord.

Everybody has an opinion some of them are good, some not so good. People love you, so all the suggestions, all the advice, all of it comes from a good place, a caring place, a place of genuine concern.... however, it is not coming from the throne of grace. Where you are walking at this moment, God's opinion is the only one you need to hear.

I will forever be grateful for the 7, as I call them. Each one of them said the same thing in the same order, Christian and non-Christian alike. It went like this, "Girl you got what?! Do you need me to catch a plane out there? You will not die from this. I have a peace and a knowing that this is not unto death" Seriously! Each one of them said those same words. Each of the calls ended with "I am praying, and I am a phone call / plane ride away." After the last call, I finally got it. This is not unto death. Now my children were saying, "Yeah mom, but it's still cancer" But God had spoken, and He confirmed it out of the mouths of 7 witnesses from seven different walks of life in seven different states that have known me spanning seven different periods of my life that THIS WAS NOT UNTO DEATH. If anyone is speaking anything other than life to you during this fragile time of your journey, move them to another place in your bubble, because what you need to hear is what the Lord has to say concerning your situation.

If you won't accept any other spirit from the devil, why will you accept fear

The Lord deals with me in dreams and visions. So, it is no wonder that this area of my life got really active during this new season. One particular night, December 12 to be exact (I looked in my journal to be more accurate) I was in that place where you are not sure if you are asleep, but you know you are fully awake and aware. You sense that the surrounding atmosphere has shifted, so you are alert and looking to see if it is a messenger from above or beneath, so you know whether to receive.... or not.......

Anyway, I saw a manifestation of satan. He was kind of like a santa figure, but I knew who he was. He reached in his bag, and he handed me murder. I refused it vehemently. He dropped it on the floor, reached in his bag and pulled out riches with a tag saying compromise attached to it. Again, I refused. He dropped it on the floor. He pulled out acceptance (clearly playing hardball with me tugging on one of my fleshly desires) but again I refused and again he dropped it on the floor. He pulled out adultery; I passed it up. He pulled up lying again I refused. I mean, I was getting tired and weary of the repetitive nature of this vision. There was nothing in that bag that I wanted. There was nothing he could tempt me with. I am resolute about my walk with Christ. Then it happened. He pulled out F-E-A-R. The fear that cancer was going to kill me, the fear that I was going to be alone, the fear, the fear, the fear. I dropped to my knees, bowing my head ashamed as I reached out to take it. The Spirit of the Lord spoke so loudly that I dropped my hand before touching it and He said, "If you will not accept any other spirit from him why in the world would you allow that spirit to overtake you" Wow! Talk about a reality check.

God has not given you the spirit of fear, but of love, power, and a sound (strong) mind. Fear is a spirit. Like any other spirit, it needs your permission to gain access to your inner man. Oh, fear can be in the atmosphere all he wants too, but he cannot enter you unless you grant him access. So many times, we focus on the top 10, as I call them, that we absent-mindedly grant access to something that we have not detected as an actual spirit.

Right here, right now, with the news that you have received, fear is trying to cloud your faith, cloud your resolve, cloud your walk, and cloud your relationships. Oh, he is a cunning and crafty spirit that hangs out with doubt, speaking lies asking you how God could allow this to happen to you, how are you going to make it past this moment, and how is your life supposed to be based on this situation, this new juncture of transition in your life. But he is a liar and the father of lies and you have to know that there is nothing in your life that God has allowed that He has not graced you to see through to the end. Understand the grace of God and withstand the crafty pull of fear so that you can be strengthened on your journey.

The Lord wants to make a covenant with you.

I never sign my name on a contract that I don't take the time to read all of the words. I don't care how well I know you. Actually, it's the private practice discipline in me or maybe it was because my dad was cunning and crafty, and my mom warned me not to be fooled but I believe in "Informed Consent" I need to know what you are offering and what I am required to bring to the table to be a recipient of it. I believe in "common vocabulary" and "non-interpretational language." That gets me in a lot of hot water with people who want me to just follow the herd, so to speak, but it has kept me out of many situations that God never wanted me to be involved in. I bring this up because as I learn more and more about my Daddy God, who I call the Lord, He is very clear and concise concerning Himself and His word and His intentions toward us. Never is that clearer than when He made His covenant with Abram in Genesis chapter 12. It became real in my life in a conference I attended 11 years ago as of this writing. There was something that I needed to know. I had to understand the parameters of this covenant.

I knew what was required of me was:

1.) *I must not stop preaching. No matter how I felt, no matter if I had just left a treatment, no matter what was before me. I would not use this diagnosis to keep me from God's Word and ministering to His people. In fact, there is a picture of me at a retreat that I keep as a reminder of this covenant. I had just left treatment with my son Wayne, got out of his car and into my daughter in love Alexandria's car to go minister at this retreat. Boy, oh boy, was my body aching, and I was cold even in my bones. Well, I preached that opening word and then asked Alex for a blanket because I was so cold. The Lord then alerted me that there was someone in need of deliverance. And the picture is of me at the altar wrapped in a blanket, bringing deliverance to that woman 4 hours after treatment.*

2.) *I was not about to stop praying. I was over the noonday prayer at church while on a journey of teaching prayer even my prayer life was on fire. I could not stop. Sometimes I went to sleep praying and woke up praying in intercession for those that the Lord was dropping in my face and my spirit. People that I still don't know to this day. I remember one day thinking, Lord; you know I am in treatment for cancer right, but the intensity and the volume of prayer that you have me doing is mind boggling. It was during this time I ministered at a prayer breakfast and forgot all about protocol and called a prayer line and my Daughter in Love told me I prayed for 137 women that morning. Really, God? But that was one thing that He required of me as a part of our covenant.*

3) *I could not stop praising. Now I'm a praiser and dancer from my belly. But boy oh boy was I praising during this time. I would praise until sometimes I was on my face before the Lord. One service we had a guest preacher and my family who didn't get my covenant with the Father because after all "Mom, it's*

still cancer" they moved to sit me down or otherwise intervene as they would sometimes do. The guest Apostle said to the church, "Leave her alone! Let her praise God! She has a mandate from God to give Him praise." It was like they were telling me the only thing I was allowed to do was cry, because they were not privy to the covenant between me, the Lord, and my writing journal. But HE Spoke loud and clear for Himself and for me. After that I was FREE to do whatever.

He spoke to me, and boy were there some things that you might think are crazy, like the cheeseburger diet hahaha. I had no appetite but around month 3, The Lord said I want you to eat a cheeseburger a day. Now there was only one place that I even considered eating a burger, and that was at the McChord AFB Bowling Alley. So, I said Jr, "let's stop by the bowling alley and get a burger". This happened every single day for two weeks and then the Lord said, "It's ok to stop" What I didn't know that the Lord knew was that my protein level and some other level was so depleted that the doctor was contemplating starting an additional protocol. But God had promised that if I was obedient to what he said that protocol would not be my portion, and it wasn't. God's part in the covenant was that none of the side effects from the treatments would come upon me... and it didn't. I never lost my hair, I never lost weight, I never had to get a prescription for pain. I have nothing to say about my brothers and sisters that have to indulge in medical marijuana for their pain. I only know that on my journey, that was not an option.

I need to tell you that God is true to His word, but you have to understand what He is saying to you. Case in point, I shared with one minister at the church what God had said to me regarding the side effects from treatment and His Covenant to me. When February arrived and it was time to begin treatment, the minister said, "I thought God said you didn't have to do treatment. Maybe you misunderstood" My reply, "Get behind me Satan!"

First, that is not what I said and that is NOT what God said. What He said was as long as I kept up my part of the covenant, He would not allow any side effect of the treatment to come upon me. He never said that I would not have to go through treatment. He said I wouldn't have the side effects. This is another tactic of the enemy on your journey to use leviathan to cloud the atmosphere so that the communication is off.

You have got to hear and understand what the Lord is saying to you in your current situation. You can't make it be more or less and you can't fine tune it to fit you comfortably. He is the Lord, and He means what He says, and He says what He means, and the manifestation comes when we are in alignment with His word. I also strongly encourage you not to enter a state of imagining what this manifestation will look like, because the flesh still influences our viewpoint. Our God's thoughts are higher than our thoughts and His ways higher than our ways and what we may see will always look totally different from His lens. So many times, we have bailed out of situations because we have seen it our way in the flesh opposed to seeing it God's way in the spirit. I will talk about that later. For now, it is important to understand that God wants to speak to you concerning this journey that you are on. He has some guidance and guidelines specifically for you. It is a personal covenant just like the one He made with me... just like the one He made with Abram.

While reading this book, you may feel lost. You want to help your loved one you want to be there for him or her, but they are not cooperative. You are quoting scriptures and praying, but they are telling you they want you to use other scriptures. They are telling you that your prayers aren't working in their life or in the situation. Oh, they may not be saying those words, but you can tell that is how they are feeling. You are trying to cover and comfort them during this season, but he or she just insists on doing things you fear will make the outcome of the journey, not what it should be. I get it. But I want to close this chapter by speaking to your heart.

Yes, you are the domino that is tumbling down, and you may feel you are spiraling out of control. The news was devastating to you, however; it was not your news. These next few weeks, months, or years are going to be nothing you thought you would be a part of. I ask that you keep in mind that this is their journey. I know you want to support and cover, but that won't be your job in this season. You may even hear from God concerning their journey. Just remember you won't be part of that personal covenant with the Father. This is not your journey that you are going through, it is only your journey because it has touched your friend or loved one and while he or she appreciates you on the sidelines cheering him or her on, you cannot walk in it with him or her. They need your prayer and your presence, but that's all you can give during this time.

In case you are concerned about what you perceive as reckless behavior or a state of denial, sit down with them and ask them if they have made a covenant with God, and if they would be willing to share. I promise you if they share it with you, it won't make sense to you, and that's because it's not your covenant, your journey, or your promise.

What should you do then? My advice to you is to go to God the Father concerning how to walk through this valley with them. Ask Him for His word for you concerning this situation. There is a purpose for you, or you would not have been caught up in the whirlwind that came because of the bad news. There is something that God wants to use you to do. You simply need to tap into it. When fear tries to grip you because your mom (that would be me ?) is praising God like she is 18 years old and you are tired of just watching her, there must be a promise from God for you to fall back on so that you will not be a stumbling block but a helpmate. Remember that help is not support if it doesn't help. Your intentions may be good, but are they God's intentions? Ask God how to minister, what to say, and how to say it. Ask Him what His covenant looks like with you.

2

DON'T BURY ME UNTIL I AM DEAD!

"Whereas ye know not what shall be on the morrow. For what is your life? It is even a vapour, that appeareth for a little time, and then vanisheth away." James 4:14.

Wow! "That was some news that shook you to your core", is what I said to myself. I had to step away from the computer as memories flooded over me. Whew! I get it. I want to do something here that I probably may not do again throughout our journey together... but then again, I might I am not sure. One thing I know is that in this chapter, I am speaking specifically to those who, like me, heard words like my "little hiccup" as they called it, which could end my life. I am not denying that you have broken your marriage covenant or that your spouse said they wanted a divorce or that you may never walk again or even that your child has died (flashback to my Candace. RIH).

These types of situations bring pain that, unless a person has experienced it, they can never wrap their mind around it. That pain for the moment may feel like it is going to kill you, but it won't. We process, we adjust, we adapt, and we keep living. It is different and it may be traumatic, but we will live through it. For those of you who have just entered the battle with friends and family, being the dominos who have just been impacted by the news, I want to share my heart on an even deeper level in this chapter.

In my situation, the "Egyptian that I faced" required a very aggressive treatment protocol. I went to school but let me tell you one thing, all that went into becoming Dr. Patti went out the window when it was happening to Dr. Patti. Let's just be real. What I knew was that life was going to be a 90-10 combination. Ninety percent would be in my mind, heart, and attitude and the other Ten percent medical practices. I understood that the best of care wouldn't matter if I died before even starting. This is why I only told 7 people. Only 1 of them lived close to me in my state. She would later reciprocate the same call that I gave her, "I just wanted to let you know that I have cancer" "I'm telling you because you are my sister and friend who I know will pray" That's it. There was nothing else to say. The marching orders given, and it was time to go into the battle.

I am sharing this because an end-of-life diagnosis brings with it a sense of hopelessness, helplessness, and finality. This is where my daughter, by way of a ring, Alex,

comes into play. She took part in one of those uncomfortable conversations that you will read about in the next chapter. Ours brought exposure to the plan of the enemy sent to destroy our relationship before it began and the covenant we made together from action and love. I just got a little misty eyed with that memory. She is about as tenacious as I am and as stubborn as I am as I talked to her. "Alex" I would say, "I want this for my 1-year cancer free party" "When I celebrate being 1 year cancer free, I want this" Her answer "That sounds good" or "Let me write that down in case you forget." It was never tears in my presence (but Abby my granddaughter told me "Mommy was crying after she hung up the phone with you") Ah.... pardon me, this one was huge for me because she never let doubt or fear or contradiction cross her lips when speaking to me.

I hadn't had the first surgery yet and there she was with me planning my 1-year cancer free party. She was driving me to ministry engagements, and she would give me this look that says, "Don't push too much farther" but she never said, "You don't need to be doing all of this." I can recall one engagement where I sat down to catch my wind and someone else continued the prayer line and this child stood in front of me so no one could get to me because people were literally stepping around the person standing in my place trying to get to me. But she didn't say "Stop Mom, sit down" She may have frowned a time or two when I sat down at engagements, and someone came up and kneeled by the chair and I ministered... but she said nothing. Why, because she heard me when I asked my family not to bury me before I died.

There were breakfasts and lunches with my husband that I hated because I would look in his eyes and see sadness, fear, and grieving. As much as I wanted to be with him, amid resenting all the time that his job required, he made time for me, and I still hated it. Why? I WASN'T DEAD! I needed his strength, but I couldn't deny him his fear. I have known him since I was in the fourth grade. I married him right out of high school. I had carried his last name longer than my parents. He was trying to figure out what December 29th held for him, and I couldn't share this with him because to do so was to put myself in the wrong headspace to fight. I needed him to be a warrior, not a grieving widower. God, I hated those meals, but they were so precious to me, even now.

My daughter, who had just got back from Afghanistan, was fever-ishly trying to get a humanitarian reassignment. I mean, like she had just finished debriefing, that's how fresh her return was. She had her own things going on but still... "Little Bit," I said to her, "I thought you liked it there. You're doing such a good job at writing your story" she said, "Mom, I just need to be there in case...you know." I told her, "Come home for my one-year cancer free party" she then replied, "How about I come home now, and we watch Dirty Dancing and The Bodyguard..." (her voice trails off and you hear the unspoken "for the last time" or "in case it's the last time). Here I am trying to be my typical over invested mom making sure that she is getting the best psychological return from war care because I know about these disorders of war. She was shutting me out because... I have cancer and I might die. Slam on the breaks! Thank goodness it wasn't part of the conversation. It was unspoken but yelled loudly in silence because... That would have put me in the wrong headspace to fight this Egyptian.

The boys, well, that's an entire book in itself. Michael would look at me about two minutes when he came to pick up the babies and leave the room. I don't know if he knows it, but I saw every time the tears welled up in his eyes. Everyday at 11:30, when he walked into this house, he fought emotions, yet he would not take his children home. He found a reason to stay until his brother arrived. They whispered, and his eye would fill up with tears. If I called him by his childhood nickname, he would have fallen out, but his heart was breaking. And then came the words, "But it's cancer mom" "Mike, don't bury me until I'm dead" Wayne said very little. He just watched. Every time I looked; he was looking at me. I'm in the kitchen making holiday treats. He's looking at me. I'm wrapping up gifts or asking him to take me to the mall (I hate freeway driving)... he's looking at me. I'm bringing the laundry basket upstairs and he's looking at me.... "making memories" AAAAAHHHH-HHHHHHH!!!!!!!! I am not dead yet people!!!!!!!!!!!! You are all grieving and thinking about what life is going to be like without me and I AM

STILL HERE!!!!!!! I need you to believe with me. To trust God with me. To plan this one-year cancer free party with me.

Now my heart is breaking because I can't fulfill my role in the family because to do so would be to feed into what has come to destroy my ability to fight. It was a terrible time. I realized more than ever that I was in this thing alone. This one was not a "When one goes, we all go family event" I had to live in the face of death and that was a hard place to be. As a sister in the Lord once said about me on her show, "DEFY HELL BY FACING DEATH AND REFUSING TO DIE" Yup, that's how she introduced me.

Why did I want to share this with you and your loved ones? Because while no one has the authority to put an expiration stamp on you and prophecy when you are going to die, on this journey, this battle with this diagnosis, it is 10 percent medicine 90 percent headspace and heart attitude I need you to understand that. It's important that you believe me. God made a covenant with you, and I need you to walk it out. I had to remember that God said that the Egyptian that I see today I would see *No More Again Forever*. He did not say that the Egyptian was going to usher me into heaven. I was not going out without a fight, and you can't either. You can't give up and give in to the diagnosis. Do what makes no sense to your human mind. It is not denial. It is fighting for your life. Not one time did I not think that cancer was not in two places in my body. I knew it was there. It was my body. But it didn't have the right to take my life. Not without a fight. Not without my best efforts to defeat it.

I remember the conversation that made Michael utter those words, "But it's cancer, mom". I was telling him about my job, asking me if I wanted a leave of absence. Shoot in my mind, the surgery was over winter break, and the students wouldn't be back in the classroom until after my 6-week checkup. Why was this even an issue? I was venting about them treating me like my life was over. Now that I have told you what Michael said, "But it's cancer mom," I will tell you, my response. "Michael, the only thing that changed on December 1 was that I had information. On November 30, cancer was in my body, and I was doing my life, so why now that December 1st happened am I suddenly supposed to not be able to do life. The only difference is knowledge and if knowledge means suddenly, I have to not live, then I wish I had never received the information." That's what I want to share with you. That condition, whatever it is, was in your body long before it came to the light. As long as you are aware of it, you must not let it stop you from living don't stop fighting.

What has changed for you domino people who read this book since you became aware of this disease, this diagnosis. Shouldn't you have already been taking the time to make memories with him or her? Shouldn't you have been sharing moments of your life? Please take the time right now to reevaluate the placement of people in your bubble because it is hard to hug a memory. The sound of the voice fades over time, as does the scent of perfume. Everything that you wish you had the time to do before.... make sure you do it today. All the things that you wish you could have done, given, and said...do, give and say today while it is day. Don't wait for your loved one to be braced for the fight of his or her life before you remember how much they mean to you and their place in your bubble. And when you make it to the other side of this "little hiccup" as the doctors like to call it, make sure that you continue remembering that Life is but a vapor. Here today. Gone tomorrow.

Thanks to the Holy Spirit and His active role in my life, I received a reality check that is still dealing with this chapter and, hopefully, a bridge to the next. It was three days after the diagnosis when we went to the Christmas tree lot, a tradition with my now grown children. Then we have tree trimming parties. Personally, I prefer Mike and Alexandria's house because of her incredible lasagna. I get pizza for our house, hahahaha. Anyway, we were scouting out the lot and that day it hit me.

This may be my last Christmas with the family. Boom, I mean, it shook me to the core. Well, I told you I knew it was happening; I had just determined to fight. I felt the tears and lump in my throat and reached for a tissue when suddenly it was like everything was in slow motion. Immediately I thought, "girl, you're having an out-of-body experience." Then just as quickly I said, "get a grip, the Lord is trying to tell you something. Look, listen, you are going to need this." I, with my bright self, said, "What is it you want to tell me, Lord? I'm listening," Hold on to your seats because this took me straight out and put things into perspective for me. My prayer is that it will do the same thing for you. The Lord spoke to me and said, "Look around you. Look closely at each one of those people. This could be their last Christmas too and cancer has nothing to do with it" Whew! Did you catch that? A diagnosis does not define you. You are defined by the purpose for which the Lord sent you hear for and the assignment that he placed in your hands... NOT YOUR DIAGNOSIS.

3

IS THERE RED IN YOUR LEDGER

A few years back one of my former students messaged me and said, Dr. Lott, when are you going to put all of your quotes into a book?" "For every class that I took with you, you had a different quote every night (9 in all) and never repeated the same quote twice." "Here is a secret, I never took classes with you so I could learn the text information, but because of the valuable life lessons you taught." Contrary to what that student said, those that know me... really know me and have spent time with me will tell you I am repetitive when it comes to ministry. I really want everyone to know the following:

1. *You were a thought that the Lord had for work on this earth that he wrapped in the womb of a woman and sent to fulfill that job.* He saw you throughout time, saw that many people needed YOU, and to fulfill their needs, you were born.
2. *You were sent here with purpose, filled with purpose for a purpose.* When you really understand what it takes for conception to oc-

cur... like really... you understand that there is a specific reason you are here. Oh, you may not have actualized it yet, but trust me and I will not give a biology lesson here just hear me when I say that there is a reason it is called the miracle of conception.

3. *God has the most amazing plan for you.* The problem is that we try to interpret that plan through our fleshly intellect rather than our spirit, so if it doesn't make sense to us and it doesn't make us feel good, then we tend to attribute God's work to the devil.

4. *It doesn't matter what it looks like. It doesn't matter what it feels like. It doesn't matter what it sounds like. It doesn't matter what people do or say. This is the day that the Lord has made, and I am going to rejoice and be glad in it.* I tell you during my journey with cancer I would often say if I dropped dead today; I am going to drop dead praising my God. And finally.

5. *I got too much red in my ledger from the sin I committed before the cross redeemed me. I can't afford to see my savior with anymore.*

And that is where I want to speak from in this chapter. You see, after receiving a diagnosis and prognosis, they placed me in a holding pattern awaiting surgery. I realized I had places to go, people to see, things to do before I saw the Lord. Did I have red on my ledger because I neglected to have uncomfortable conversations with people that I needed to have? Were these people in their current state because I was too focused, too driven, too busy with Patricia-Eileen's life to tend to any business we may have had. Was I so busy building a deliverance ministry that I had neglected to minister? Had I become so hardened by the responses of people that it was simply easier not to talk to them than to deal with the pushback they gave me naturally and spiritually? Is the work I do and the purpose for which I was created, planned, and sent fulfilling the purpose for which I was created? Wow!

And so, to prepare for what was to come, I took a deep breath and had a series of uncomfortable conversations. It got to the point that it is still a running joke in my circle, "If First Lady invites you to lunch and says that she is treating, make sure it's not Reyna's" The reality had sunken in that if I didn't do this now, I may never have the opportunity to do it again.

The bible says in numbers 11:29, "And Moses said unto him, Enviest thou for my sake? Would God that all the LORD'S people were prophets, and that the LORD would put his spirit upon them!" Many of those conversations began with the word. I wish more than ever that you could hear that you have a condition that is so aggressive that it is likely to kill you within a quarter of a year. Even though I did not wish cancer on anyone, it is sobering to realize that you can't put off any longer what should have been done already. The reality that tomorrow is not promised to you.

Now I know people role play scenarios about what would you do if you knew you were going to die at such-and-such time. But for me, it was not a role play; it was a reality, and I did not want to plan a trip. I did not want to travel back to Philly to see my family. It was not my intention to write that novel or do anything grandiose that you could imagine. I wanted to make sure that my family was ok but more than anything in this world; I wanted to complete my assignment. I wanted to remove the red from my ledger. I had places to go (mainly to Reyna's); I had people to see (those uncomfortable conversations), and I had things to do. With 21 days to work, the work of Him that sent me because on the 22 day it may be that I no longer had time to work. I went at it with a vengeance now that is not the right word, but I was definitely passionate about the message.

I know the Lord speaks to me concerning others. Since I was 23, I have been an intercessor. I would have people brought before me to pray for and then the Lord confirms it later through various ways. I can speak to the crowd, but the Lord wanted the one-on-one evangelism, deliverance, exhortation, comfort, and ministry to take place.

The scripture says that when you see your brother overtaken in a fault, we who are spiritual are to restore such a one. Why hadn't I restored? In fact, why didn't I follow Ezekiel's teaching when I saw my brother or sister heading in the wrong direction to tell them. Wouldn't that have prevented them from falling and needing restoration in the first place? Well, I was not going into surgery with that red in my ledger. If these three sets of seven days were all I had left, then so be it. I was going to be found doing my father's business.

It is at times like these that one discovers who they really are and what they really believe. I was not fearful; I understood the covenant, but I also understood that I had slacked off on my assignment.

In this moment, let me ask you who is reading this, when the news hit your ear-gate and you realized that the course of your journey had changed. Did you press into your purpose, or did you get swallowed up in the situation? I am not passing judgment on anyone, for we are as diverse as the hairs on our head and our fingerprints, but I have found that for us, being the son and daughters of God, rarely is He our first thought or priority when these situations occur. If you did not get instructions on how to proceed from God, who gave you permission in the first place, how could you go through correctly?

Let me give you an example. There was a woman that I will call Jane. I have not heard a single positive word from her since I met her some 11 years ago. She talks about how strong of a Christian she is. She talks about her gifts, talents, and calling. She is always negative, however. Her perception is that people are always out to get her, treating her badly even when her behavior is questionable. Anyway, back to the point. Wouldn't you know the Lord called me to have an uncomfortable conversation with her? And wouldn't you know that I just didn't want to because of the negativity? Between the time I called to speak with her and the time we spoke, she lost her apartment, moved in with her mother, and then her brother returned home. He was into ungodly things. But she attempted to superimpose her values and her representation of Christ on the family in a legalistic way, exposing her religious spirit, and it caused her mother to ask her to leave. She found herself in a shelter.

When we met at the restaurant, she went on and on about how awful the shelter was and how she shouldn't have to be there. How the devil was just wreaking havoc on her life. How God had just turned his back on her and that's when it happened. That's when the Lord said....open your mouth and have the conversation. I asked her didn't you say, "Yes God you can use me, in any way you see fit?" "yes, but how am I supposed to be used by him in a shelter?" My question to her was "Did you ever stop to think that the Lord had orchestrated you being in that shelter so that you could reflect him to the women there? Have you ever pondered the fact that your whining and complaining and constant murmuring on about the great victim you are gives no one any hope? Who wants to serve the God that you portray?

Paul said, "Behold, I show you a more excellent way" he says that we are not as those who have no hope. You may be in the same situation that the other women are in, but it's how you go through it that is going to draw or repel others to the Lord. Who have you drawn to the Lord by how you live day after day? The things that you do, the things that you say and how you think? If your life is an epistle read and known of men, what have they learned about God after reading it? Had the Lord not done anything in your life? Oh, she got angry. She told me she would leave if it wasn't for the chance to have real food instead of shelter food. I smiled and said, Jane, "I will still pay for your food feel free to get a To Go Box, but before you go right here, right now I want you to tell me one good thing about being a Christian. Tell me one thing that the Lord has done for you." After about 5 minutes, she gave an answer. A rather superficial surface level answer, but it was an answer. I asked her to tell me something else.

Then I began to recite her experiences since I had met her and after each thing I asked her, "Who protected you? Who made that come to no end? Who covered you?" I went on to say, "when did you forget our God is so very faithful? When did you spiral to a place that you would prove to the Lord that your 'yes you can use me' was actually about you dictating where, when and how?"

The food arrived, and we ate in silence for about half an hour. Then the tears and the just above a whisper "Lord, forgive me for not being content with simply being your daughter, for wanting and demanding more and then pitching a fit when it didn't look like I wanted it to" "Forgive me Lord for not making good use of my time." "Forgive me God because I see it was because of me that this one and that one and the other one (I just don't like using people's names) want nothing with the church, the body of Christ or you. I was so blinded by my hurt and hate that I didn't see what I had become." For the next half hour, I sat quietly as she was delivered through her honest conversation with God. Simply because instead of avoiding her like so many others had, including me, I had the uncomfortable conversation. Just something to think about.

There are missed opportunities because we have the wrong priorities. There is an old saying that says don't put off until tomorrow what you can do today. For someone reading this book, you just literally came to the realization that there may not be a tomorrow, so you need to do it today, while it is day. These opportunities I had came when I took a deep breath and asked, "Answer me this, if you were to die today, if the doctor said to you today that you are going to die in one hour, is your soul really prepared to meet the Lord in peace. Here comes another one of my sayings, "Listen we are all going to go to heaven but not all of us are going to get to stay." Are you going to stay, or will the Lord say depart from me I never knew you or worse yet, ye worker of iniquity?

Pretend I am God for just one minute and tell me why I should allow you into heaven. These were hard conversations because we don't like to face the fact that our walk is not matching our talk. As much as we remember where we found the Lord, we have no idea where we left off following him because we are holding on to old testimonies instead of tending to our salvation on a daily basis. Twelve or thirteen uncomfortable conversations took place. People were hurt. People were angry. People faced the truth, which is never easy. But it was necessary to save a brother. To win one for the kingdom.

I am speaking to someone right now. You have red in your ledger. There are people you were supposed to look in their face and minister the kingdom to, no matter how they may look. People who were assigned to you for you to bring into the kingdom. There are places you know the Lord told you to go and cleanse or anoint with your presence. Places that the Lord told you to grace and bless. There are things He told you to do, like write that book to bring healing and deliverance to the nations, record that song or encourage that neighbor, cover that latchkey kid, or intercede for that couple struggling to remain married or intercede for that unknown girl caught up in prostitution or that boy in that gang, that addict, you know what it is.... You have just been putting it off. But do you really want this red in your ledger?

The good thing about your situation is that you have a gracious and loving Father who hasn't taken you to the depths of no return without giving you the opportunity to complete your assignment. If only we were not like Jane, spending time dwelling on the situation and circumstance instead of using the time we have to accomplish what we were sent here to accomplish.

So now I need to talk to you domino people. I know you are feeling hurt, confused, let down and left out, but there is a reason. Your loved one realized the clock is ticking, and the alarm is about to sound, and then they will have to give an account to the Lord. As much as he or she loves you, they have a mandate to fulfill. In other words, we have to give up some time with you for the welfare of the kingdom. I know you don't want them to be found wanting or lacking when they stand before the righteous judge. Let's use our imaginations for a moment. Please humor me. We are all at the judgement seat of Christ and your loved one is at the foot of our Lord. "Why didn't you tell Bobby about what his lifestyle was doing to him and where he stood in the body of Christ?" Why didn't you tell Tracy that she has worth and value and to stop selling herself to men and that I was reaching out to her?" "Why didn't you walk into that outer court and bring my cleansing word to the temple" and then you hear your loved one say, "Lord, my family was upset that I wasn't spending time with them that could be spent tending to the last things. They didn't want me to do it, so I didn't because of my love for them" BOOM! How does that make you feel? Do you hear the Lord asking him or her "Lovest these more than me?"

I know it is hard. I have been the daughter whose father had laryngeal cancer and dying who was determined to live. I have also been the mother and spouse with the diagnosis that said I might be called to leave here. All I wanted was more precious time with my dad. I wanted was to please my God. Your loved one is in a hard place, but they must work the work of Him that sent him or her while it is day for when night comes, they can no longer work and there will be red in their ledger that you cannot erase.

You will be complicit if you stand in the way. Panic is setting in. Every moment of every second is cherished to make memories you can hold on to. I get it. But and this is a very big, but... this is not your journey, and this is not your mandate and while it touches you it is not about you. What your loved one needs is your understanding your support and your strength. If there is a drive that you don't understand, if there is a passion that you can't seem to wrap your mind around, then take a minute and imagine what it must be like for him or her. Oh, how they long to be with you, but they long to fulfill their assignment, whatever it may be. They are constantly faced with the reality of their mortality. Finality is ever before them. The reality of "good-bye" is ever before them. They must adjust to the reality that their lives have changed forever. Pray for him or her. Intercede that they have the strength to get that red out of their ledger and still be able to spend as much time with you as you desire while allowing you to be all the things, they need from you.

I also want to leave this thought with you in your walk on this journey called life. The clock is ticking for you too. Many of you do not keep that in front of you because "YOU HAVEN'T HEARD THOSE WORDS"

Are you so busy making a living that you stopped making a life? Are you so busy with frivolous pursuits that mean nothing except satisfying your selfish desires that you are about to abort or, worse yet... miscarry, the very thing that God has for you? Are you putting it off until you reach a certain milestone, pace, benchmark, believing you have plenty of time, that God understands that it's ok because eventually you will get around to it. You know! When things ease up a little, when things get better. Well, I have some sobering news for you... You are amassing an incredible amount of red in your ledger.

In my heart of hearts, I believe that this is why Moses uttered those words in the beginning of this chapter. He understood the magnitude of the job that he was sent to do. He had to follow God's timing and not his own. It was a massive job to him because it was his job. Not so with his siblings, or they would have kept their mouth off of him. Not so much with the children of Israel. All they cared about was that they were out from under the hands of the taskmasters. It didn't matter to them; they didn't stop to even consider what great a price Moses was paying to bring them out. So, he uttered those words... "I wish that for just one minute each one of you could carry this burden, then... then... your life would be different."

This is why I said in so many of those uncomfortable conversations, I don't wish cancer on you, but I wish that you could have those words spoken into your ear gate, then and only then will you be able to realize that you got places to go, people to see and things to do. You must work the work of him that sent you now, while it is today, because you can't do this work from the grave. Your loved one knows it because they heard the words. So how about it? Even though you haven't heard those words, how about praying your loved one through and follow suit and begin to get rid of the red in your ledger?

4

⚜

KINGDOM CONVERSATIONS

And the hand of the Lord was there upon me; and he said unto me, Arise, go forth into the plain, and I will there talk with thee. Then I arose, and went forth into the plain: and, behold, the glory of the Lord stood there, as the glory which I saw by the river of Chebar: and I fell on my face. Then the spirit entered into me, and set me upon my feet, and spake with me, and said unto me, Go, shut thyself within thine house. Ezekiel 2:22-24.

I start this chapter by dropping you at the end of perhaps one of my favorite chapters in the Bible because it was during this time that this passage became real to me. Not that it wasn't real before, but it became real in the sense that the one who said, "I am the Lord I change not" did not use something new as He had with me a series of what I call "Kingdom Conversations"

Before I delve further into this, let me share a few definitions with you coming from the KJV Dictionary:

Plain -Smooth; even; level; flat; *without elevations* and *depressions.* Open; clear. Void of ornament; simple. ***** *Honestly undisguised; open; frank*; sincere; unreserved. Not obscurely, *in a manner to be easily understood.* Distinctly, articulately; as, to speak plain. Mark 7. With simplicity; artlessly; bluntly. Easily seen or discovered; not obscure or difficult to be found; ****** **Field of battle.**

Glory of God - The manifestation of God's presence as perceived by His people. The *experience* of God. Experience - something personally encountered, undergone, or lived through.

Like the Prophet Ezekiel, I understood and was familiar with the presence of God... or so I thought. I found out on December 19 that I had been in his presence most of my adult life, but I had not experienced the glory of God personally. I am not talking about when His glory cloud descends in the service, or I get lost in worship; I mean like experience Him in that He took me out of myself and filled me with Himself and to this day I don't have the words to tell you what happened, but I know that I never want my life to return to where I am not in that place to experience Him.

Like Ezekiel, the Lord spoke to me and said, "Patti, put on your coat and get a pillow and sit on the stoop. I need to talk to you" Sitting there the presence of the Lord began to manifest Himself to me in every way that the definitions above describe. I understand why you read that people fell out as if dead or fell on their faces. It was all I could do to focus and remain cognizant of what was happening. Funny, to my husband looking out the window, nothing seemed unusual. To my neighbor it just appeared that I was sitting on the stoop, but My God, what was happening. The Lord initiated a new meeting place for He and I to have "conversations" He said that he wanted to commune with me. Me, Patti, the girl from West Philly who lived on the wrong side of 52nd Street and Market Street. Me, Patti, who always seemed to be on the fringes, never quite fitting in anywhere I desired to be with whom I desired to be. The one always in some sort of trouble or bringing some sort of disappointment to someone. A person who fought for everything. The one who shed the silent tears of a Pastor's wife never fitting the mold of what people thought it should look like.

I am so serious when I tell you it was told to my face that I need to stop traveling and running revivals all over the place, sit myself down and get a hobby like a prayer breakfast or tea of something like a good Pastor's wife should. Someone to whom it was said on more than one occasion: "Oh you're that kind of evangelist" Me, Patricia Eileen Beverly Lott.

I asked, "God, you want to have conversations with me?" In this place, that is nothingness, yet everything all at the same time. Me? The tears of worship are flowing even as I try to get this across to you and I feel Him stretching me to hold a little more of His glory. So, my prayer closet remained my kitchen, but my Meeting Places for my Kingdom Conversations became that stoop and the top of my staircase. I'm not kidding.

Moving on, the first conversation that the Lord had with me opened up to me that I needed to understand that while I was not special, I cannot be like anyone else. He began to open to me that there were some things that could no longer be a part of who I am, what I do, where I go and with whom I associate. He shared with me that there were universal no no's, there were leadership no no's, and there were personal no no's. I use the phrase no-no because, as the Lord explained, not that it is sin per se, but that it cannot be tolerated nor accepted in my life.

There are some things that once you surrender your heart to Christ as your Savior and yield your body to Him as your Lord that regardless of who you are, they will no longer be named among you. Then there are those things because I was called and anointed to walk as a teacher, preacher, evangelist and the "P word" as I called it then, cannot be named among me. However,.... Because He called me to be who He called me to be, and he expected me to walk in the places He called me to walk. In the series of assignments and mantles that were about to be a part of me, there were specific things I needed to be aware of. They might not seem major to you, but they will cause me to miss God's plan for my life.

Talk about blowing my mind. Talk about tears flowing. Here I am, 10 days away from surgery and the Lord is telling me that there are things in my existence that He is not pleased with. I have been having these uncomfortable conversations, walking in expectation awaiting manifestation, staying true to the covenant, living all that I know (you may not know me, but some people who are reading this do, so you understand what I mean about standards and no compromising).

God spoke plainly about my attitude and my thought processes. Let me stop here for a minute because I need to go a little deeper. His exact words to me were, "I give people free choice and free will. Who are you to take it away from them" Now let me tell you, that has gotten me in more trouble with "God's people" than you could ever imagine. He told me, "I want you to LOVE people back to life, love the devil right out of them" Boy, would that one be tested. God talked about the way I would just shut up and shut down... but he knew my thoughts. Whew!

In all honesty, it felt like more than 15 minutes that I spent outside, but let me tell you something: I was so enveloped by the grace of God that it didn't matter. The Lord began to deal with me about the way I would do my head, the way I looked at you with a cold, steely stare.

On that stoop, he made me another vessel, said, "I have something to tell you, and I want you at the place I can tell you. "So, remember that while I don't have a problem when others do these things (I haven't even scratched the surface of the list) I will have a controversy with you if you do." It was as if the Lord washed over me. He empowered me through His presence and words.

Kingdom Conversation: "What is it that you need from me today," "Lord, I need for you to help me not complain because I feel that often what I say can cause people to feel some type a way. To not be so passionate about my walk that it leaves others feeling condemned or as if they will never measure up," "Let's work on that today,"

Kingdom Conversation: "Patti, draw close I want to show you something that I spotted behind your third rib, three layers of the bone down. We have to work on that today,"

Kingdom Conversation: "Come up here into my glory. Flow without the constraints of your feelings, your past, or your mindsets of how it is supposed to be and Just be."

Now I have to explain why that was something that I will never forget. When my husband started pastoring our church. The Lord spoke to me and told me I was to go into the sanctuary for 7 days during my lunch break and sit. Well, I tried to pray but he would say, "Sit" at the end of the week He said, "Seven more days." So, I tried cleaning. He said "Sit" on the 30th day He said "Remember this. This is what My presence feels like right here in this place. If any other manifestation shows up here, you will know and you will be able to take authority over it because you have learned what My presence feels like in this place." No matter whether it is high praise or worship, teaching, fellowship, I can feel His presence. I learned that His presence was not about the singing, the praising, or any of those wonderful things that happen at church for us to say it was good today. I learned His presence. Now He lifted me into His GLORY. I got to experience Him and Jesus.

There were times that I would sit, the fragrance of roses saturated the room. People would ask what perfume I was wearing, I wasn't. I blessed some oil for my first prayer clinic and people are still talking about the rose smell. It isn't me, it is God's Glory, the Glory of the Son. He taught me about the Rose of Sharon, the beautiful rose that thrives in challenging climates and seasons. He taught me about the simplicity of salvation and gave me a mandate to bring it back to that simplicity. Oh, there are not enough pages in this book to share what these conversations did and taught me, but I will say this, that first encounter I was shaken, but on surgery day, I understood even during treatment, and the first year of recovery, I looked forward to my Kingdom Conversations.

These conversations ushered me into a deeper relationship with the Father and a place in the spirit that I never, ever want to forget. One day Poppa Rob as we called him at church said to me, "First Lady, you are glowing so I can hardly even look at you" and before I could reply he said, "Did you know you are walking in the glory of God?" Whew!

Last Kingdom Conversation that I want to share before speaking to your heart. It took place on December 24, at 9:45am in the morning. The Lord said "Patti, I want to teach you about Grace today," I came out of the kitchen and sat on the top of the stairs and said, "Here I am Lord," "What is Grace?" "Your unmerited favor to me," "No, Patti, it is *My presence, My power* and *My favor **gifted*** to you," "Listen, you have a lot to learn and a little time to learn it," A lot of details are confidential so whoever gets to my journals first, they're in for a treat.

"The Lord said to me, You said 'Yes' to Me when I asked if I could use you and I took you at your word because you have proven to Me, I can trust you. I have an assignment for you because of that, yes. It has already begun, but it will be very hard for you. I want you to know that every assignment I give you, I also gift the Grace to complete it. I don't want you to walk through this assignment being anything else than Patricia-Eileen. I will do the rest. Don't try to figure it out. I don't want you to try to help Me out, just be you. I've been creating and re-creating you over the last few weeks. My grace is sufficient for you. I have gifted you with the grace to complete this assignment."

I still wasn't sure what was to await me, but two things I knew for sure. This cancer was a part of my assignment which was in response to my "yes" and that whatever was to happen, the Lord had gifted me with His presence, His power, and His favor to complete the assignment. He gifted me grace.

Many times, we walk through life giving God the measure of ourselves that we feel comfortable giving. Since we have done that, we believe everything is fine. When we are diligent not to commit the top ten sins, as I call them, we kid ourselves into believing there is no sin in our lives and heaven is automatically our home. We do a memory dump about all the "little foxes" that have come in to destroy our vine. We forget that just because we are Christians doesn't mean the work is done, for He tells us in John 15:1-2, "I am the true vine, and my Father is the husbandman. Every branch in me that beareth not fruit He taketh away: and every branch that beareth fruit, **He purgeth it**, that it may bring forth more fruit.

There are things that are named among us that must be dealt with. No longer can we be like the man beholding himself in the mirror, forgetting what he saw when he walked away. But God wants to bring you in closer to Him. God wants to commune with us. He wants to reveal Himself and His glory to us. He wants us to be carriers of His glory and not carriers of our self-will and self-ideals, self, self, and self. So much self that no one can see His glory.

You have heard the words, and your life will never be the same. God has covenanted with you concerning the words he spoke to you. You are working feverishly to get that red out of your ledger. But are you having conversations with the Father? If this sickness is not unto death and God honors your struggle and says LIVE, what are those things that you need to tend to? I had a mouth on me. In one minute, I could have my husband thinking he was superman, and the next he couldn't even formulate his words. I would whip out that Doctor vocabulary in an instant. I didn't care.

You were like dead to me in my mind if I didn't want to be bothered with you. Were either of those things sinful? No. Were those things weights? No. Can the majority of the women on the planet walk in that and God be ok with it? Yes, but for me.... It could not be a part of me anymore. What are some things that the Lord wants to work on in your life? Have you asked Him? Have you admitted that you are tainted in His hands? Did He tell you, but because you were religious, legalistic, self-righteous, or in denial, you didn't or couldn't hear Him? Were you the hold up all along of the manifestation that you longed for from the Lord? Today is a good day to meet God on this Plain. It doesn't have to be a stretch of land. It doesn't have to be the stoop or the top of the stairs. It just needs to be the place where all the distractions and obstructions have been eliminated. It needs to be a level field where there is no title, designation, or position. A place where a visitation from the father can take place.

Maybe it was easier for me to step out of the box because my relationship with God has been nothing like traditional. My mother raised me in the church and my testimony is that sin found me in the House of God. Some things that I am most embarrassed and ashamed of took place in the church. But when I surrendered my life to the Lord, it was in a schoolyard. I didn't fall out under the power of God in the arms of ushers who laid me softly on the carpet and covered me with a sheet. I hit the concrete ground covered in broken glass, but when I got up, Hallelujah, with one glance my mother could tell that something had changed in her daughter.

Perhaps it is because I never got involved in religious traditions and have little patience for religious spirits that the Lord could talk to me on the stoop. I don't know, but what I do know is what he said. He had a special assignment for me. God has an assignment for you, too. Inquire of him concerning this length of your journey ask him to step into you and commune with you and prepare you for what is to come.

Having the covenant is not enough. Whatever you do, you have to walk right, since God has gifted you with the grace to complete it. You just have to believe it, receive it, and keep it stirred up along your journey. God is waiting for you to position yourself for his arrival. He is willing. Start a Kingdom Conversation with Him Today.

INTERLUDE

A PAUSE FOR THE CAUSE

God is so good and so gracious, and I just want to take this time to tell Him thank you. I mentioned earlier that this was not one of those where one goes, we all go Lott events where I was alone, but I was not alone. I had to walk this journey alone.

Christmas eve I will never forget. I was sitting in the office (the place I hide in my house). Wayne was doing something with his dad, and I was thankful that he wasn't watching me. I was tired. I felt my strength fading, and I whispered, "Lord, I need a conversation with you. I'm a little scared. I want my little girl." For those of you who don't know, she is my hero. I said, "I need her strength and courage. This is a girl thing! I just wish my little girl were here." He said, "Ask me." I said, "Lord, I know that with you all things are possible. If I have found favor in your sight on this Christmas. This Christmas of uncertainty, I sure would like to have all of my children here with me. Would you please send me little bit of grace home?" Now, she is going to be angry that I put her nick name out there. But that is what I have always called her... "My Little Bit of Grace," and these were my exact words.

I knew that Mike, Alex, and the babies were going to come over later, so there I sat in my office, no brave face, no pretense, just allowing the Lord to strengthen me to get through the night.

I hear a key in the lock outside the door of my office. I think to myself, "That Wayne locked himself out of the house" I shook my head and wiped my eyes because what he wasn't going to do was to see me crying. That would have taken him all the way out.

In the house walked my daughter!!!!! Won't God Do it!!!!!! I let out a scream that brought both of the Wayne's came running to the office. She said that she was home until a week after the surgery. She was on leave and wanted to surprise me, so she drove home... for Christmas. Well, those tears got to flowing for real then. I asked Him, and He provided. Just like that. That Christmas Eve, all of my babies and grandbabies were here. It was perfect... except for that date looming over everyone's head but mine. I was so happy so in a place that for that brief moment in time, I was not hearing those words ringing in my head.

It's December 28. I am coming to the end of about the hardest year of my life. My father passed away in February, 2 months after my mother-in-law passed. Between Wayne and I there were no more parents. There'd been a scare with my daughter in Afghanistan, but thank you Lord after those awful three days ... But here I was about to go into surgery in the morning. Mike had taken off of work, the Wayne's had taken off of work, Alex had taken off of work, but I wanted to be somebody's little girl. I wanted something that was once nuclear that had become extended; I needed home. But wait. I was the oldest. Man!

As Jr and Little Bit played Halo or something, I just laid there. Just give me that feeling of home, Lord. Why did I tell my sister/cousin Betty not to come? Why did I tell my girl Grace not to come? What is wrong with me? I needed family. I needed that bloodline strength, not that married strength. I wanted my family. I heard my mom, "Wayne is your family now" I thought to myself "Shut up you know what I mean" Just then Wayne walked in and laid down beside me. "Oh man, this is not going to go well. I'm in tears, and he cannot handle that right now. What am I going to do?" I felt him pull me into his arms and I turned my face to the wall.

"Lord, I want my family. I need a connection from home. If I am going to do this." He said, "Ask me" I said, "Lord, can you please give me the strength to call my brother and not freak him out, even though it's like 1:00am in the morning where he is?" Father said, "I will do better than that, just for you" I laid there trying to compose myself to make this call. There is the sound of the house alarm and I am like who is coming in my house at this time of night it's 10pm? Mike says, "Look who I found at the airport" It is my brother!!!!!!! Won't God, do it????!!!!!!!! Y'all, know I screamed and jumped out of that bed. He says, "I'm here Sissy. Get some sleep you got to have your strength in the morning." And just like that, a sweet sleep fell over me.

I found out something else. On this assignment, because of the magnitude of it, not only did God gift me the grace of it, but he also gave me access to a place where he responds immediately whenever I pray. To this day, I am careful when I pray for people or when people ask me to inquire of the Lord on their behalf. I will always say, "Are you sure this is what you want." You have looked at it from all angles, no surprises? Sometimes the Lord says, "don't ask Me that", but most of the time when I ask God for it, it is going to happen.

I still wasn't sure what was to await me, but three things I knew for sure. This cancer was a part of my assignment which was in response to my "yes", as I travel down the road of this assignment when the need arises, all I have to do is ask and whatever was to happen, the Lord had gifted me with His presence, His power, and His favor to complete it. He gifted me, **Grace**.

Last stop at this length of my journey. On December 29, I arrived at the hospital early in the morning with my husband, my three children, and my brother. I remember that time as the craziest of my life, and yet every time I think about it or even write it, there are tears flowing, but they aren't all tears of sorrow and here's why. I check in and the nurse says to me, only one person can be with you. I look over at this group that I know Oh so well and say to her "You tell them that because I am not going to even waste my breath" She does, they politely say, "OK."

Well, it is time to go to nuclear medicine, guess what... each one of them get up and off we all go to nuclear medicine. Which was wonderful, because I had to send for my daughter to come into that room with me. To this very day, if I go to that section of the hospital, my breast goes into some sort of spasm and the pain doubles me over. I have an aversion to nuclear medicine, and I will leave it at that.

We travel through the hospital and at each stop they say to my family, "Only one of you can accompany her" At each stop the entire troop files in with me. I am so hoping that they all stay on the correct side of the cross because I have seen what happens when pushed to the other side. I am so serious and at that time my daughter was not professing salvation and did not even care and that is all that I am going to say about that. I had just seen a side of my brother at our father's funeral and that is all that I am going to say about that. While riding in my wheelchair I prayed, Lord, I can't handle it if they go to acting out of character, which by the way, no one in my family allowed any medical personnel to push me. (SMH)

I was ready to be wheeled into surgery, so I guess the news of my family and their total disregard to the one-person rule had gotten there before us because they had space for all of us as they lined up beside the bed. There was Sr and my brother who are close to my heart. As they positioned themselves next to me, Mike was standing next to his father and Jr was standing next to him. Little Bit was standing right by my head. My brother was standing guard at the foot of the bed.

This was it. Boy, was it an atmosphere of nervous anticipation so thick I could almost see it. I was like, "Lord, there are three preachers beside my bed (Wayne, Wayne Jr and Mike). Why is it so thick in here?" The Lord said, "I am here" I prayed, "I need more" His reply was, "Ask Me" "Lord, please speak out loud and drown out the noise coming from the silence" "Ask your husband to lead the family to a quiet place by reading my word out loud." I said, "Wayne," he said, "Yes." "Will you read to me from the bible?" While waiting for me to be wheeled into surgery, as a family we were reading the word of God together. It was so powerful and empowering.

The anesthesiologist came to see me. He was NOT who they introduced me to at the meeting. He was not on the team. God had blessed me with a saved doctor who was an associate minister at his church. I had a saved radiation oncologist, a Christian anesthesiologist who was a deacon, I had a recovery nurse who was assigned to me who was a Christian.... what was this? This was not a part of the plan. I felt a shiver of panic. I said, "I was expecting _____." the anesthesiologist answered, "Oh, he won't be with you today, you will just have me."

I began to cry. "Momma, it will be ok" then Mike looks away. He couldn't handle the tears. "That steely look that sees straight into your soul from Jr followed by "Mom, God's got you" my brother then spoke up, "Go get who is supposed to be with my sister right this minute. You are not working with her. You already have her upset" More tears. Wayne is squeezing my hand and brushing the tears off of my cheek, not saying anything. I think he just couldn't handle my reaction. Why was it all falling apart? Why was there a breach in my hedge and why right now? Little Bit of all people said, "Fam Bam, let's pray" and so the family began to pray. As they prayed, I felt the peace of God flood over me and I hear Jr's voice, "God's Got You" and then I was ready to go through those doors alone to begin the hard part of the hardest assignment entrusted to me by the Lord in my life.

I still wasn't sure what was to await me, but four things I knew for sure. This cancer was a part of my assignment which was in response to my "yes", as I travel down the road of this assignment when the need arises, all I have to do is ask, that whatever was to happen, the Lord had gifted me with His presence, His power, and His favor to complete it and that God had me. He gifted me with Grace.

5

WHEN YOU SAY YES TO THE LORD... BE PREPARED

Jesus answered, "Neither hath this man sinned, nor his parents: but that the works of God should be made manifest in him." John 9:3

I make no apologies for what I am going to be saying in this chapter because I believe that the body of Christ needs a wake-up call and a reality check. When most people say, "Yes Lord" What they are really saying is "Yes I will accept the call to preach or pastor" "Yes I will feed the hungry, write that check, donate that item and otherwise do whatever it is that I want to do because I am somehow special and more gifted and anointed than people acknowledge" That is stinking thinking, and it needs to be exposed and exercised so that the works of God can be to be manifested throughout His vineyard.

I have maintained that cancer in my body was a direct response to the "Yes" that I gave the Lord and so during this length of the journey I want to talk to you a little about 7 people, a willing vessel, and a Great BIG GOD.

I dropped you off with the introduction of a different anesthesiologist, so that seems like the place to pick this up. He was stop number one or the first part of this assignment.

I heard singing while I was in surgery. It was the song that has become the signal that I am about to move into a spiritually supernatural experience or manifestation with the Lord. I rarely think about the song, but when it resonates inside of me, I begin to check all the boxes to make sure that there is no hindrance from stepping into the assignment. It is important that we rest here for just a moment in this experience as to why this song is going to play a major part in what you are about to read. If you know it, sing along with me if you don't know it, maybe one day the Lord will have me sing it over you.

The song goes something like this, "*Miracle working, Jesus, I need a miracle. Miracle working, Jesus, I need a miracle. Miracle working, Jesus, I need a miracle. Miracle worker. Work a miracle. For me*". I heard this as plain as you are reading this right now, as I was in the operating room. I just didn't know it was me I heard singing the song.

My surgeon came to see me, and he said, "We got all the cancer out. Technically, you are cancer free, but to make sure you are going to have to go through the treatment. Blah blah blah all the medical stuff concerning the types and stages etc." He says he will see me at post-op.

This where things get crazy. So, he tells me, "Thanks to you we have a new brother in the body," I'm like "what," with the side eye. He says "yes." "Remember the family emergency that landed you with a different anesthesiologist?" I'm like "yes." He said, "I had never worked with him before. He was from a different section of the hospital. You were having problems breathing. I told him to take the seal off and put the tube down your throat. This is where our amazing God showed up. After placing the tube in your throat and making sure everything was fine, you young lady began singing loud and in a perfect pitch. You sang all the way through the surgery." (Hit the brakes. Stop the presses. Hold the phone. You mean that wasn't the angels or the surgical staff singing, that was me? Back to the assignment).

He goes on to say that the anesthesiologist says to him, "Sir, I think I have just witnessed a miracle. She is singing with a tube down her throat." I tell him, "Son, you have just witnessed two miracles. You see this image of two places of cancer? Well, look here, there is only one place of cancer, and it is not aggressive in any way. That second cancer is gone. The cancer was there in nuclear medicine just a couple of hours ago, but it is not here now,"

The Doctor (oh how I wish I could release their names, because they were the most important people in my life... still to this day) relays the following conversation that took place over me, to me. The anesthesiologist said, "I guess God is real after all." My Doctor said, "Oh yes son, God is real," the anesthesiologist said, "You know Sir, my girlfriend was a bible thumper and she died on deployment in January. Everyone kept talking about God's got this and God got that, but I just didn't have a need for Him. I didn't believe in Him. I said to God You have 1 year to prove to me you are real. If you do, I will apologize for not believing and serve you the rest of my life, I was prepared to wage war against everything that looked Christian since I felt God didn't care about me, if He were real,"

Let me interrupt this conversation for a minute. This guy gave God until December 31 to prove he was real. This was December 29. Whew, I feel like running around this office right now. OK, I'm back in my chair in front of this computer and back to the conversation. The Doctor said, "Well son, not only did God give you one miracle he gave you two just in case you tried to back out of your agreement." The anesthesiologist said, "Sir," the Doctor said, "Yes," the anesthesiologist said, "Do you have some time after this surgery to tell me more about God? I wasn't scheduled to work today, but they called me in for this one surgery because they didn't have anyone to fill in for it." The Doctor replied, "Yes, son, just let me talk to the family, clear the rest of my morning and we will go have something to eat" And just like that the Doctor told me, this young man gave his life to the Lord.

Because God orchestrated things, this anesthesiologist was in the operating room and was the one to put the tube in my throat himself, so it was not what someone told him, it was what he witnessed for himself, seeing from the scans and inside my body that the cancer had been removed, and that they had gotten all the cancer cells they could identify, he experienced this for himself. He didn't overhear it in the cafeteria, he wasn't talking to some friends, and it came up. The Lord God spoke to him for Himself through that cancer surgery.

There is someone out there right now whose soul lies hanging in the balance. Life has thrown them a curve, and they don't know the Lord you serve. They are without hope, and don't know how to place their hope in God. You may be tempted to be all in your feelings and fears about what is happening in your life right now, but the Lord wants to use this to manifest Himself in the land.

He needs to trust that your yes and your resolve won't disappear because it is not looking like what you thought it would. God has to use this thing to get you to the place that he needs for you to be in order to accomplish what needs to be accomplished in the earth. There is a reason that you have been selected to carry out this assignment. Seriously! You may be about to go to divorce court and don't want to be divorced. Trust me, God is trying to reach someone who needs your influence to reach their heart in just the right way. There are some miracles that He wants to perform through this, even if it is his will that your marriage be restored. So, what if the divorce went through, that doesn't mean that the Lord will not bring you back together as a part of his manifestation in the earth? Yes, you are grieving over the loss of your child. Lord knows not a November goes by that I don't think of Candace, but there is someone in the middle of this that the Lord is reaching out to. They don't know the Lord like you do. They need you; God needs you. That's why He trusted you with your Yes.

Listen, this young man wasn't going to anybody's church. He wasn't reading anybody's bible, tracts, daily bread, absolutely nothing. He wasn't around anyone who could minister grace and truth to him. Even his surgical unit was of such that he was not around anyone strong enough in their faith or with sharp enough discernment to pick him up in the spirit. But God wanted him, needed him for work in the kingdom and so with a tube down my throat and a preacher for a surgeon, Heaven won, hell got robbed of a soul.

Moving on to stop number two in this assignment. Same hospital. Same day while in the recovery room, I am somewhere between unconscious and conscious; I hear this singing. This miracle working Jesus. Work a miracle for me.

Then I heard a voice that brought me straight out of this in between state. It was my Little Bit of Grace asking, "What is wrong with you don't you see my mom leaking? You'd better do something." I look up and I really don't know what is going on, but she is telling me, "Come on, Mom let me help you get dressed. I'm taking you out of here this makes no sense." I'm like, (that special pet name I call her, Lol) "I need a moment to clear my head."

Then the nurse says, "I am so sorry. I know it has been longer than they said, but you just don't understand," my daughter replied, "And I don't want to understand. You had us all scared and junk and for what?" I then replied, "Shush Little Bit!" Then something happened that I hadn't expected. This precious woman that I had only seen once at the family briefing and introduction of my care team and never again since, wipes her eyes and I realize that this puddle of wet on me is her tears.

However, always the psychologist I sit there in my daughter's arms and let her talk. She tells me she is broken and lost in her church. That she had simply been going because it is what you do when you are a good Christian. She said she hadn't felt the presence of God in months and that her relationship with the Lord had started to weaken. (then enters lucifer who sent a man designed specifically to rob her of her identity) and was struggling and didn't have anyone to talk to because all the people saw her as was a good Christian girl who had it all together. She shares how she is scared to talk to them because of the critical and judgmental attitudes of the leadership. I then feel my daughter tensing up, but she knows her mom, so we listen.

The nurse continues, "Then they brought you in and as I sat here watching you and waiting for you to wake up, I realize you are singing. It is low, and it is soft, but you are singing. I ask the Lord to let me feel Him like you, to let me know He is still with me. Father, I want to experience your presence" she continues, "each time you sang that verse, something else inside of me broke and not like in breaking me apart, as months and months of stuff began breaking off of me. I sat here in the presence of the Lord, and I got lost in worship until I'm guessing this is your daughter came in. I am so sorry. I am so sorry".

You reading this please know If I wasn't fresh out of surgery, I would have ran around that recovery room, prayed for her and we would have had church... but then again... she had better ran around that room, she was the one who had been ushered into the presence of the Lord. While there in His presence at his feet, HE DID THE REST. All I had to do was be me through the process.

I often sing my prayers. It is something that I developed after my mother passed away. She was always singing and now, so am I. As she came to help me dress, my overprotective daughter said that she had me. When I came out, I took her hand, and I whispered a prayer to her, and she thanked me.

"Mom, can you stop being a preacher for one day? Can you just get through this cancer stuff?" "No, I can't." See, the covenant with the Father was not to stop praying, not to stop praising, and not to stop preaching. To do whatever God spoke to me... this was part of the covenant.

So, I need to speak to the Domino People again right here. Your loved one heard the words spoken by God. The person you once knew is changing and becoming and there are going to be things that you just don't understand and may not like. There are going to be times you mean well. If you are not careful, you will stop what God is trying to do through them in this situation. It is unintentional, and it comes from a good place, but you can't allow where you are on your loved one's journey to stop the assignment that they are on.

Please know that since God has given them this assignment... He has gifted them the grace to complete it. Your loved one is just as apprehensive about the immediate future as you are, more so, but there is a place that you are not a part of where a strength that does not come from you is infusing him or her and moving him or her in ways that you have to be careful not to get in the way of.

For you completing the assignment, it is hard when those you love want to take care of you and you want to just rest in their care and just heal; however, you understand it must be completed even in your weakness, not your strength. Just remember, "God's got him or her" as well.

When I think about the nurse, assignment number two, as I am writing this, I think about John 4:4 "And he must needs go through Samaria" I had to be there in that recovery room. Why? So that someone who was crying out in her innermost being for a fresh wind and fresh fire, someone one who felt alone and lost, could find her way back. I must needs go through the hospital because someone was crying out to feel the presence of the Lord and the Lord wanted her ushered into His presence to do His work. My assignment.... get her there to His presence.

So, let's head over to stop three of this assignment. To do so, I have to move out a couple of months later when a man walked into prayer and said he had been looking for me for months. I want for you to put a bookmark there and remember what I said the man walked into church and had been looking for me. In his words, "I came upon your picture on your church's webpage, and I knew it was God."

Now if my family isn't anything else, they are protective of their mom. So, I had to give the side eye and proceed with caution because some crazies have walked up to me at the church house when I was in my full strength, SMH lol.

So, he introduced himself as a pastor. He began to give his testimony where he had been in a car accident and it severed his spine, and the verdict was that he would never walk again. He was in the recovery room with me. Go figure. He said that he was a faith preacher. That is how people in the area knew and referred to him, the preacher of faith. He had stirred up faith in so many people he had lost count. His words not mine. I had never heard or seen him before.

He shared that laying in that recovery room with the wheelchair next to him, knowing that he would never walk again, he was composing his resignation from the ministry and the church. He actually said, "Here I preach faith and my life was about to be spent in a wheelchair." He continued testifying, with his x-rays in his hand.

He said that he could hear me singing and bitterness began to form in him as he was angry at the turn his life had taken. The more I referred to the miracle working Jesus, the more the stones built up in his heart and he said within himself, "Well you sure didn't work a miracle for me. Did you?" He said at that moment I sat up with my eyes still shut, pointed at him, and said, "Hey Preacher, Don't peddle a product that you don't believe in," and I laid back down. He said that his recovery room nurse explained to him that I was still unconscious and that it was a reflex, and it was normal. But he said that it shook him to his core and his stomach flipped. God had used me to call him out. He preached faith and yet when it came to his walking again, he didn't have faith past that wheelchair. He said he wept and repented before the Lord.

Now, let's loop back around to the beginning of the encounter... This pastor WALKED into the church. He wasn't wheeled in, and he was not in a wheelchair. He had medical proof his spine had been severed, and he was the walking proof that, according to your faith, be it unto you. He said no one would give him my information at the hospital (Thank God for HIPPA laws) He said that he just needed to look at me and tell me about the change in his life because of my "reflex" in the recovery room.

Then a friend was telling him about this woman who ministered to his wife at a retreat and that she had this mad crazy faith like him and maybe we could fellowship sometime. He looked on the church web-page and there I was and so he came, just to testify about the goodness of God calling us out and set us back on the straight path. Hallelujah! Thank you, Jesus. Unfortunately, I was notified as I was writing this book that he had died as a result of the coronavirus, but praise God, he walked until he walked into heaven. We serve a great and mighty God, yes, we do.

There is a place that I call the place of "Crazy Faith" the kind of faith that everyone in your bubble thinks is delusional or so out of the box that they can't comprehend it. My son Wayne Jr has that crazy faith and a little later you will read about how that came into play with my journey. Crazy Faith is a place that believes God when common sense and uncommon sense say not to.

It is a place that dares to repeat God's words back to him, expecting not hoping, not wishing, not wanting but expecting him to do exactly what he said, no matter how out of the scope of reality it may be. I phrase it like this when I am talking to people. I live with expectancy and therefore I walk in manifestation. Every person who has heard those words in whichever form they came has been given this opportunity to access that type of faith and walk in that place. It is a glorious place. It is not a place for the fearful or faint of heart. Life or death, victory, or defeat, standing or falling are all decided in this place. The haughty and arrogant have never been there, for no one is humbler than the person who has heard those words. It is where the gifting of God's grace is all that you can see, feel, think, hear, and receive.

Please Sir, please Ma'am, hear my heart. I know those life changing words devastated you. They pulled the proverbial rug out from under you, and you are fighting just to exist, but there is a greater war that is going on in the heavenlies. There is an attack going on regarding the core foundation of God's people. These weapons are fear, discouragement, hopelessness, helplessness, frustration, and hurt. In the midst of your fight, there are people you will be introduced to that you will empower and strengthen to hold on just a little tighter, a little longer. It is you who will shake them back to reality by refusing to lie down and give up.

There is a spiritual war going on for their faith and their place in the kingdom and believe it or not, this person you meet is losing that war. He or she is like that pastor, ready to give it all up and walk away. It is your refusal to live by the rules of this low place, but steadfastly occupying the place of crazy faith that gives the enemy of their soul that knockout punch, so to speak or to give them just enough life-giving air to revive them and get them back in the fight.

They are in a place where they are lost because the enemy has just that much of a stronghold on them. But you, in your lowest, most vulnerable state, are being used by the Father to walk into their life to shake up the atmosphere and break them free. Yes, You. Why? Because you said, "Yes Lord, you can use me" and the Lord took you at your word. You can't give up now. Too much is at stake. And here's the thing, you don't have to be or do anything except BE YOU! God will do the rest.

Next stop (#4 and # 5) on this assignment was oncology. Now, listen, I am familiar with the spirit of Death. My first encounter with him was at age five as I knelt down on the floor next to my grandfather in prayer and he took his last breath. I experienced him again at the birth of Michael when he stood in the door to the delivery room beckoning to me and then my husband would see his shadow as he jumped over me.

I have moments when I can tell that the death angel is about to move in my atmosphere, whether I know the person or not. I had never experienced such a strong sense of death until one appointment I had in the medical oncology clinic, or whatever that place was called. I called it the realm of the dead. Death was everywhere. My spirit was so disturbed.

It was here that I had to revisit this covenant with the Lord. It is ok to do that; you know. I needed to reaffirm to see if we could make some changes because I just could not handle it. So, I am sitting in the waiting room, which is smack dab in the middle of the realm of the dead. There were rooms to the left, rooms to the right, rooms behind me, elevators, and a door in front of me. The stench of death was so strong. I shudder just remembering and telling you about it.

Wayne Sr is on one side of me saying something. I couldn't hear him. Death was trying to swallow me up. I could feel the vomit welling up inside of me. To this day, I believe I heard death say that he finally had me. It was awful. Anyway, I couldn't lean into My Guy as I called him back then. I was trying to find a way out of this place of death. Wayne Jr was seated on the other side... watching me. He could see death suffocating me. I wish he would stop looking at me all the time. It is as if he is in a different place, much like me. It is unnerving to me.

Finally, he said, "Mom, You OK?" shaking my head no. I said, "I can't do this, it's too much. I can't survive here!" Jr says, "Mom, God's got you!" I was thinking, "What is taking so long. They are half hour late and the longer they wait the more death is enveloping me." I felt death's breath. I felt his touch. Literally, I felt him reach out, stroking and taunting me that finally he had me, and he was going to drag it out, torturing me until I begged him to take me.

Death wanted me to give myself to him. I kid you not. It was this heavy demonic presence of death surrounding me. I knew death couldn't take me unless I gave myself over to him. Tears and silence. My husband goes and talks to someone. He didn't do well seeing me cry. He came back and said come on.

We walked into this office and once again I was introduced to someone who was not on my care team. We were told that he was in the room with someone who was transitioning. Oohhh, I hate that word "Transitioning". Why couldn't they just say dying. Ugh!

Focus, Patti! She introduced herself to me as the chief of oncology and said that she was personally going to take my case and apologized for the wait. A tormenting spirit had joined the group. I don't know what that woman was saying because I pressed into the Lord. I was like God; "I can't do this. I don't want to fail you, but I can't do this. I need you to strengthen me and sustain me if I have to. If I have to, I'll say yes, but please, if there is any other way, please Lord, deliver me out of the realm of the dead".

The peace of God overshadowed me, and resolve stood up in me and right about then Wayne Jr says, "Wait a minute can you explain that again so I can be sure what you mean when I call the family" (See he was the mouthpiece. I never made those calls to the children or sibling.... He did) I was so glad he said that because I missed the whole thing I was in real warfare.

The doctor goes on and explains that she doesn't know why the surgeon ordered the test he did and that normally they don't order that test. She said that as long as she had been at the hospital, or in the field of oncology, more specifically, she had never seen this particular test ordered, even by my surgeon. The results, "The damage from the medical oncology treatment would be more damaging to me than beneficial, so I recommend that your mother not do this treatment. I am going to double her radiation oncology just to be on the safe side".

The crying in the waiting room was the most emotion I ever allowed My Guy to see on this journey... or so I thought. I grabbed him and hugged him. Wayne Jr filled with emotions as well who's my rock. Rubbed my back, in that rub, I heard "God's got you!" Walking down the hallway toward the elevator to leave the realm of the dead the Lord spoke and said touch that door and pray.

I laid my hand on the door and prayed that the Lord be a testimony of Himself in the life of the person in that room. I asked him to stay the hand of death on the floor. If for only the rest of the day, that the grip of death be taken off of the person on the other side of the door. I guess the Wayne's thought I was passing out or just overcome with emotion, but they stood as pillars keeping me steady. Then we got in the elevators and went home.

Here is where the assignment manifests, about a month into radiation, the oncologist who was supposed to be my oncologist wheels a gentleman into the waiting area. He looks at me then says can I speak with you for a minute? I'm like sure. What's up? Inside I was saying, "Satan the Lord rebuke you, God said I didn't have to do test. I refuse to receive from this man if he tells me; it was some sort of mistake and I have to go and take that test."

He says, "I don't know if you know who you are, but you have brought me down a few pegs and I owe you, well, I owe the God you pray to an apology." I'm looking just as confused as I can be. At this point, I don't even know what is happening. "You see," he said, "That day you came to begin your treatment, I was in that dying man's room. I have become sort of an expert on when the patients are about to die, and I was standing on the other side of the door when you prayed through the door" I heard you and I laughed.

"Foolish woman" I said, "That's about the dumbest thing I have ever heard. We sure do get some strange people up here, but whatever works and helps them get well, you know." He says, he starts filling out the death paperwork when the patient, are you ready for this? It took me all the way out! The patient sneezed and woke up. It is almost as if the sneeze blew the residue of the disease out of his body, and he made such a quick turnaround that he is able to join you here in radiation." What?!!!!! Gllllooooooorrrrrrryyyyyy! Hallelujah God did it as a testimony to himself.

This oncologist, while not ready to receive him as Savior and Lord, acknowledged that my God was God. Do you hear me? The oncologist said that he regretted he wouldn't get to work with me because "There is something special about you." "Oh no Sir, I'm not special I'm just a little girl from Philly trying to get back home to heaven to my daddy."

Psalm 23:4 says, Yeah though I walk through the valley of the shadow of death I will fear no evil for thou art with me. Thy rod and thy staff comfort me. Despite the intense evil tormenting spirit that was present, the Lord was with me. I had to go there on that day at that time for that manifestation. I wrestle with trying to understand who was the actual assignment, the man who had death broken off of him or the doctor who had to come to the realization that there is an intelligence higher than him, and that no one not even him has the authority to place an expiration date on anyone's life. Death and life belong to the Lord, not man, and in my wrestling, I have come to realize that they both were the assignment.

I want to say to you right now that not everyone that you come in contact with or that the Lord allows you to meet is going to be receptive at that time, or possibly ever. You have to know that you are just the tool that the Lord is using, and the choice ultimately belongs to that person.

On a side note, I went to my 6-week appointment with the surgeon a week after the realm of the dead experience. I thanked him for the test. He looked surprised and said, "What test? I honestly don't remember requesting it when we sent your tissues off." "Well that matter is too high for me, God knows what He is doing doesn't He" I replied. He said, "YES He does!!!!!!"

I believe my intense, honest prayer in which I voiced my fear, taking back my authority over me coupled with my willingness to say nevertheless even in the midst of it all that My God wrote in my records that day and worked yet another miracle in this body. My surgeon didn't even know what I was talking about, but I know that God heard the cry of his obedient servant. I believe that he decided I could complete the assignment without having to undergo further wrestling that day, for the yoke was destroyed, death held back and the man who thought and referred to himself as god came to see that our GOD is GOD!

Stop Number Six. My oncologist is an associate minister at his church, and it was my job every Monday during treatment to be seen by him. We had many discussions about the unusual way in which I viewed treatment. Mostly for him, it was that I only had good days and great days.

So Here is where we join this stop in the journey to completing my assignment. There was a Kingdom Conversation in which the Lord said to me, "Don't advertise for the devil, advertise for Me," Now to you reading this it may not make sense but for me I am such a stickler about giving the devil too much attention and too much airtime.

I cringe whenever my husband allows testimony time in the church because it is a litany of commercials lifting up the devil. You know what I mean, "the devil really came after me today" I try to do the right thing but that old devil...." Very rarely are people actually talking about the goodness of the Lord without the precursor advertisement of the devil. I often would pray, "Lord, when will we stop advertising him and advertise YOU?!"

So that struck a chord with me. It was the Monday after my initial visit to oncology. So, after my conversation with the Lord, I had come to the decision that I was only going to have "good days" and "great days" because the enemy of my soul have had enough of my days, and he was not deserving of not another one of them.

Seriously, to this day 10 years later if you ask me "How is my day?" You are going to hear either get, "It's a good day" or "It's a great day" "The Lord is strengthening and sustaining me" and so about four weeks into treatment (ev-e-ry sin-gle day) I walked in to see the oncologist before my radiation. He said, "how are you doing today?" "My reply, "Doc, it's a good day".

This time he stopped, and he looked at me, really looked at me and he said, "You are amazing. I know what is happening in your body. I know what is happening to your body, I look at you and you never cry, you never complain, you give as good as you get and even on days when you are leaning on your son barely able to make it to radiation you tap on the door, smile, and wave and say, 'It's a great day'! How do you do it?" I said, "Well, I didn't pop out of the womb saved. I haven't even dotted all of my 'I's' and crossed all of my 'T's'. Since I became a Christian at 16, I had a lot of growing up to do naturally and spiritually. Along the way, unfortunately, satan got too much airtime out of my mouth and my life. He doesn't deserve any more. I refuse to give him my day. Every day the Lord blesses me to be alive... it is a good day. Every day that I'm alive and not in pain, I am able to stay awake, able to go to work at night after treatment and give it 100%... That's a great day. I refuse to have any other day. It doesn't matter what it looks like Doc, it doesn't matter what it feels like, It doesn't matter what it sounds like, it doesn't matter what people do or say, This IS the day, that the Lord has made I am going to rejoice and be glad in it. It is a great day."

I didn't know what I had just done. Correction, I didn't know the spiritual battle that was just won. Just being me in my vulnerable state, I had just took authority over a suicide spirit and snatched my doctor as it were from the fire... until the next Monday when we spoke.

During my next appointment which I will never forget. It went like this, he said Patti, "I need to Thank you for saving my life." I was like, "What in the what are you talking about?" He said, "Last week I had planned to take my own life. I come in here day after day, and I find that I am powerless to make a difference. Every time someone dies from this terrible disease, I feel as if I am a failure and have let the Lord down. I had written my letters and made peace. It was my plan to leave work, go home and kiss my family and simply end it all. I was hurting so bad. We had a week where literally 7 of the patients in my little waiting area, die. It was heavy in this place. I looked at you."

He continued, "What I heard you say did not match what I saw going on in your body. When I asked you and you told me about not giving the devil the authority to dictate your day, I felt something inside of me break. I realized that for all of my faith and all of my grand way of thinking, I was allowing the devil to dictate my day. I was giving him too much air space and too much authority. I went home, and I told my wife. For the first time since being stationed here, we prayed together. I told my pastor about what you said. It is now the slogan of our church 'I only have good days and great days I refuse to allow the devil the pleasure of seeing me have any other day."

Well, you could have bought me with a penny and got change. I didn't have to pour oil all over him, I didn't have to have a conversation with that spirit, I didn't even have to acknowledge him, all I had to do was be authentically me and the spiritual warfare took place and deliverance came and suicide failed at his assignment to capture another one of God's children.

I would like to tell you reading this book that have heard "those words" Be careful of what you say. I know that there is a lot of discomfort, fear, anger, and a plethora of emotions associated with the life that those words have caused you to take. I understand that for some of you, just getting out of bed is a chore. But you are here and that is the victory. Those words did not take your life, they only change your life. Let me say that again. Those words, whatever they were, did not take your life they only changed it. You are here. You are a manifestation of the kingdom on this earth and the Lord is with you. You may not feel as if he is, but he is. Right here with you. You are not going through this on your own.

In fact, the truth is that you have walked through it all since you heard those words. Everything... everything that you have done is because He is CARRYING YOU!!!!!!!. It is because of the Lord's grace that you have not been overtaken. As much as you hurt and don't understand along with all of those other feelings. The truth is that you have the victory, you are still here in your right mind, with a reasonable portion of health and strength. You are having a good day. You have managed to complete that task, You managed to keep your head held high even if there were tears in your eyes, You managed to ..... you are having a GREAT DAY!!!!!!! Don't let those words be the vehicle that the enemy uses to snatch you away from your place in the body of Christ. The enemy can't get you, so he is trying ever so subtly to stop you from giving God worship and praise. Listen, God's got you and there isn't anything the enemy can do about it. It is a GREAT Day.

The final stop on this assignment is perhaps the one in which I truly felt like Ezekiel could have possibly felt, that my life and my body was the prophecy, testimony, weapon of warfare, and not my words. It is with this assignment that the works of the Father were made manifest through me.

Put your feet up, grab your coffee or tea or water if you are a fellow waterholic and let's begin this journey. It started the very first day of treatment. My son, who was my support person, had taken off work to take me to treatment. I had no clue what I was going to go through, but I had the promise of God... He had graced me to be successful. I had to hold on to that with everything that I had with this encounter. "Just be you Patricia-Eileen and let Me do the rest" I had to stay in that place for this entire journey.

So, I see this nice cheerful nurturing nurse and I am so happy because she came to me as everything that I was going to need to get through this. However, when my name was called, she was not my nurse. Instead, I had someone else an immediate wall went up, and I didn't understand why... but it only took 5 minutes to understand why. Her name is Jane, and she gave me permission to use her first name in this book.

On that first day, Jane began to explain the radiation process to me and take my vitals and give me the tour, so to speak. She told me that I needed to have tattoos placed on my body. "Ummmmm, no. I'm not going to do that" she said, "Why?" I told her, "It goes against my belief and my faith." Jane said, "Oh, you are one of those" I said, "Excuse me?" she said, "One of those fanatics that want to use an invisible deity to justify trying to run things down here" I said again, "Excuse me?" without hesitation she replied, "What gets me is you are an educated woman. It says here that you are a doctor, a psychologist, you should know better,"

Once again replied, "Excuse me?" Now let me tell the truth and shame the devil. I had a Philly Flashback as they named it when I moved here, and I wanted to slam that woman against the wall and beat her. I am just telling you the truth. That hit my flesh, and I wasn't trying to hear anything that the Lord was saying to me. I opened my mouth to give her a piece of my mind. How dare she come off to me like that? She didn't know me, but she is going to get to know me. It is bad enough that I am going through this. I don't know what to expect or even if it is going to work. I am battling a spirit of fear and all I have to hold on to is my faith in God. And you are going to attack that. Really? But none of that came out.

The Lord said to me, "Patti, I need you to keep your word. I trusted you. Be you and I will do the rest." I immediately took a cleansing breath and said to her," "I am not going to get tattoos. She says to me, "It will make things more time effective. It will enhance your treatment. We give them to everybody." I said, "No" she said, "Listen with the tattoos, once you get undressed, the machine it will pick up the tattoos and direct the treatment, without them we will have to position you every day and that will take time" I said, "No" she responded, "Why the... (sigh catching herself) why not?" I told her, " The bible says that thou shall not make any cuttings or markings to the flesh. I am not going to do it. It is not like I had tattoos before giving my life to the Lord when I didn't know this, but I do know now how He feels about it, and I will not do it." She said, "Fine" there was silence...vitals...doctor...radiologist techs. Then she said, "She's resistant, call me when it's time" I felt so sleepy. I couldn't keep my eyes open. I really felt as if I was drugged.

The tech takes out paper. I asked, "What's that?" The tech replied, "To lay across you in order to start the tattooing process" I said, "Oh, I am not going to be doing that" she said, "We can discuss it after we do the scan" Well I fell asleep in the scan and this nurse decided to tat me in my sleep. I woke up to a pinch and a diabolical smile. I can't explain it, but I knew I was looking at something other than this nurse. I was so done, I was so hurt I began to cry (not wailing, just tears streaming down my face) "Look no one will even notice, it will look like freckles" I told her, "God will see and I will know, and I told you no" And then the strangest thing happened. I began to pray. I asked God not to lay it to my charge that these tattoos were on my body and to forgive Jane because she couldn't understand the things of God being separated from him. Like I went into an uncontrollable intercession for her. And.. She... Got... Angry... and the war was on.

That weekend I was inconsolable. I cried, and I prayed all day Saturday, all day Sunday and Monday clear up to 2:00pm when Wayne Jr came to pick me up. I felt broken and to be honest betrayed by the one who sent me on assignment, that He allowed this had happened to me.

There was no fight in me this day, I did my vitals. I saw the Oncologist he asked, "Are you ok?" I said, "It's a good day" and left it at that. I went to the back to await my turn in the machine. I get on the table, and it happened. Jane said, "I thought we tatted you Friday." I said, "You did." She said, "Then how come there are no tats on your body?" the other tech said, "See, here is her sheet with the holes in it, we did tat her, where are the tats? Jane come see this. Didn't we tat her Friday" Jane said, "Yes." "There are no tats" Jane says, "Well missy, we are just going to have to tat you again". I said, "No missy, we shall not. What we are going to do is put me in that machine. If it picks up the track to apply the radiation, you are going to drop this whole thing. If it doesn't, then God has a reason for me to deface my body and I will willingly take the tats and we won't have any more discussion about it."

Heeeeeyyyyy Glory. They laid that machine over me, and it whirled and caught the track, and we never discussed those tats again. But Jane was very angry. So, it was everyday the same thing. Jane asked me," How are you doing?" I would say, "It's a great/good day!" Then she said, "Is the side effects from radiation happening yet?" She asked. Normally it would be something like burning, peeling, ruptures, all that cancer stuff. My answer was always "No" she said, "Are you sure?" My reply, "Yes, I'm sure." Jane said, "Well you should be experiencing this now, some of this and that's" God told me to be me and I gotta mouth that I keep at the foot of the cross. So, me being me came up with an answer everyday that was sure to send her out of the office with a slammed door. One day I told her, "Well forgive me, I never had cancer before so all I have to go by is what the Lord told me and that was I wasn't going to have these side effects." Slammed door. Shaking my head as I walked to the back to get undressed for treatment.

I noticed that there was a wigmaker there one Tuesday when I got in the room. "Hi are you Mrs. Lott?" I spoke up and said, "Great!" The wigmaker then replied, "Jane said that we were heading to the time where you should be experiencing hair thinning and loss, I am here to get a feel of what to create for you, it is free." I asked her, "Um, are we talking about a wig?" She said, "Yes, it's a part of your treatment" I replied, "Oh, I won't need it. God said," Jane interjects "yes yes God said God said, He sure does a lot of talking to you doesn't He" The wig maker look disturbed, and I simply finished, "My stylist is a Christian also and every Saturday we pray as he does my hair. I believe God that it will be just as He says."

Well, I need to let you know that not only did I not lose my hair, but my hair grew down to the middle of my back. I will never forget that Sunday when I was in my husband's office with the children, and I had not combed my hair yet because we were running late. I took my hat off, and my hair fell down and Michael said, "My God mom look at your hair" Hahahahahahaaaaa. That was a great day. That wig is still at the hospital waiting for me.

At about week 5, I noticed that there was yet a different scale in the office. I paid it no attention, as it was the fourth one in 5 weeks. That is until both radiologists came in and asked, "Jane, why do you keep ordering new scales. We got our butts handed to us by command to-day" Jane replied, "Because they are misfunctioning," they said, "What do you mean?" Jane said to him, "Her! Look at her Sir, she has not lost any weight, not even an ounce. That is impossible. It must be the scale." So, my Doctor, the Christian says, "Are the other patients losing weight?" She said, "Yes," The Doctor said, "Then don't order any more scales." Looking at me mumbling under her breath, "I know God said you wouldn't have any side effects" That day I left a daily bread booklet on her desk on my way out. She threw it in the trash.

The next day, I put a daily bread on her desk on my way from vitals to the treatment waiting area. I looked to see if it was in the trash as I was leaving. It wasn't. The next day when I turned the corner to do vitals, I saw her quickly shove the daily bread in the drawer. I said nothing, simply went into the room for vitals. The next week, I put a book of healing scriptures on her desk. I heard it hit the wall when she threw it, but it never made it into the trash. Now you may think I was being petty, but that is really me, being me.

Let me tell you about the cheeseburger diet. So, I went to treatment, and she says... huuummmmm. I say Hmmmmm what. She says, "hummm we will just wait and see what you God has to say about this." It was a Monday. The Doctor didn't say anything out of the ordinary, examined my breast, asked about church, nothing out of the ordinary...

except a quick look of concern. I just wanted to get home. It was a good day. Jr was sitting in the waiting area in the back, and I said, They sure are acting funny, "Maybe someone else died. It does feel heavy in here today." I go into get my treatment. I come out and we head home. About three stops from the Airforce base, I'm like Jr, I want a cheeseburger. Let's go to the bowling alley and get some burgers" This is significant because I had what is known as a food indifference and as far as my cancer diet was concerned I was basically drinking smoothies and allowed to eat whatever I wanted as long as I ate. I know go figure.

The doctor even said to me "Regulate, don't eliminate" Well, I had cravings for Bowling Alley cheeseburgers everyday for 2 weeks and just like that on that Friday it stopped. The following Monday Jane was a storm waiting to happen, and the Doctor is smiling from ear to ear. He asked, "What have you been doing? How was church yesterday? Did you go up for special prayer?" I told him, "Ok I was having a great day but if something has changed give it to me." He said, "Oh, you see, Faith has trumped science once again and that is great for me being the only Christian in the front. You see, your protein levels went down really low, to the point that we were contemplating changing your treatment and starting you on something even more aggressive. I told staffing, give it two more weeks whatever you have been doing is working because your levels are back to normal. It had to be supernatural" Me being me says, "No, it was my Sounder's Lane cheeseburgers for the past two weeks" He fell out laughing and he escorts me to the treatment area.

Today I found out about an undercover agent (Christian). Normally, there were two technicians in the room when I had my treatment, and it was always dark and silent. Look, I am a child of the light; I don't like to be in any darkness. This day, it was bright, and it was light as far as my mood and as I got on the table, the tech said, "What is that song you are always humming when you come in?" I told him, "It is a song by Juanita Bynum called you are great." He said, "Who?" I replied, "Well since we can't have our cell phones on in here, I can't play it, but I'll write it before I leave.

I started to sing, "You are great, you do miracles so great. There is no one else like you" He says, "That's it" I needed to hear that song. You know I am a Christian but not a very good one. I see what they put the doctor through being Christian, so I keep mine undercover." "Wow, I am so sorry to hear that. You know secretly living for him is the same as denying him. I am sure that hurts more than if you willfully sinned." He replied, "Ouch, never thought about it. I just don't want to be mistreated because of my faith." I spoke up, "Dude, have you not read Isaiah 53? Have you not read that we are blessed when we are persecuted for Christ's righteousness sake? How can you expect to ever know Him in the power of His resurrection if you refuse to partake in the fellowship of his suffering? Man, it is an honor and a privilege to being mistreated because of your faith! Well, let me be quiet. We all have to figure out our relationship with Christ. I got 12 hours to work on my relationship and 12 hours to let you figure out your own. I'll be praying for you, though. Oh, and just so you know, it makes this a little easier knowing that there is a brother in here with me... even though no one knows but me and the Lord"

Jane enters the room and I sense him tense up. "Good to see you again, Jane," I said. "Did you get a chance to read that article on faith that I left on your desk? I thought you might be able to use it since this journey is 90% about our headspace and 10% about the actual treatment. It's a good thing that I focus on my faith because what consumes one's mind controls one's life" I just thought it might be a helpful tool." Door closes but doesn't slam. The tech says, "You're so bad. (Chuckles) No, you are so brave. I want to be you when I grow up." What a day, he wasn't a part of my assignment, but The Lord wanted to stop by and see about him while I was on assignment.

I don't know what got into me, but one day I decided to leave a bible on Jane's desk. The oncologist said, "She hates you and you seem to get some pleasure out of tormenting her." Then before he came in for the exam part, he said, I pray for her, you know. She is such a great person, but she will never let Christians see it. Keep doing what you are doing, it's working if for nothing else keeping her in her office the two hours you are here" hahahaha. She came in with the bible in her hand, "Did you do this? I bet you thought that I was going to throw it away. It was probably an accident you meant to leave some other book, but I am not going to give it back. Now what do you think about that?" I just shook my head and lifted up my arm for the exam.

Fast forward two more weeks. The only thing that I was happy about going to treatment that Monday was that it was Jane's day off. She wore on me. I think I was more fatigued dealing with her on a daily basis than I was with the treatment. So, Jr and I walked into the radiation Oncology department and who is there????? Jane and she like rushed me. Like kind of aggressively. So much so that the receptionist looked up and Jr came and stepped beside me because she was told on more than one occasion to back off of me. She says with finger in my face almost touching my nose in a voice almost a growled whisper so that I think only Jr and I heard it "Your God is God and if you tell anybody I said it, you will be sorry" Yes, I smiled and I wanted to run around that clinic but ya'll I was tired. I had not been that tired through the entire treatment.

My vitals remained the same, side effects nonexistent, hair in place and longer, weight the same (I really would have been aright losing some weight though Lolol) but it was a great day. The Greatest day I felt until the next day... Wednesday. I get a call to come into treatment an hour early. Now that shook me because they drilled into me that I must get zapped with this radiation at the same time everyday. So, what changed? What was I going to have to deal with now?

I go to check in and there was Jane, and she says, "Don't check in yet. I have so many questions and I thought if you came in early we could talk before you have to start treatment. It's my lunch." I turned my eyebrow in the direction of Jr. she asked me about my certainty of God. She asked me about salvation. She had posted arrows in passages of scripture in the bible she refused to give me back. SHE ASKED ME HOW TO BE SAVED!!!!!!!!!!!!!!!!!!! Thursday as I was leaving to head to change for treatment she says, This may sound crazy, but would you pray for me. I have always wanted to do Doctors without Borders, but I am a nurse and they never have actually viewed my application.

She shared that she was a nurse practitioner, so she was comparable to a doctor. I felt like this was one of those test to see if God is who He says He is, then He will do this for me. So, when I was leaving, I was very specific in my praying that Lord, if it be Your WILL, allow this to be so. Then on Friday at my appointment I was trying to work on my puzzle in the waiting area and all she wanted to do was talk about God's will. I was so glad when a patient came in so she could leave me alone.

Two weeks later, I came in and there was another nurse. I hate change, so my blood pressure shot up. For better or for worse, at least I was familiar with Jane. "Where is Jane?" I asked. The new nurse said, "Oh she's not here but I know we will get along well. You just look so full of laughter and joy" I don't want to hear that. I want Jane. I think that was what was fueling my flame to endure this treatment. I go into the exam, "Where's Jane?" "She has resigned her commission and won't be with us anymore. She left this for you" I replied, "What the what?" She said, "Now what the who? Patti, they accepted her into Doctors without Borders!" Ahhhhhhhh. Hallelujah! Hell Lost again!!!!!!! Then she says, "You know, I think I only need to see you once a quarter for a while. You are doing so well." I looked at her and said, "Wait what?" I get back to the treatment room and there is the tech, with the receptionist, the other doctor and my doc coming up behind me with a certificate and they tell me that it takes more time to get undressed and onto the table than it takes actual treatment, and they were graduating me from treatment.

That was a GREAT Day. Assignment complete. Like I still get goosebumps. Like God said, she is the last part of your assignment. You went through it and no matter how rough it got, no matter the wear and tear on your body and emotions, you proved that I could trust you. Well Done Patti, well done.

I want to speak to your heart who is reading this chapter. God has a plan and a purpose for every length of the journey that you are traveling right now. It may look totally off the wall and like it was sent to destroy you. I imagine that is how Joseph felt at times on his journey. God had given him His word concerning his expected end. He never in his wildest dreams thought that the road to his end would lead to betrayal of his brothers, becoming a slave, getting molested by his boss's wife who then lied and had him imprisoned only to be abandoned by people whom he used his gift to help. But it did and at the end of that journey the bible declares, *"But as for you, ye thought evil against me; but God meant it unto good, to bring to pass, as it is this day, to save much people alive."* (Emphasis and underline added)

I never thought in my wildest dreams that when the Lord asked me if He could use me, and I said yes and when He asked me if He could trust me to complete this assignment and I said yes, that it would mean hearing those words and going on that journey. I never thought that I would feel such incredible separation from all I know and love, nor require a measure of faith that I didn't even know existed, much lest I would possess.

Those words were hard. Those words forever changed you. Those words changed the trajectory of your life. As crazy as it sounds, there is a purpose for it. A purpose much larger than you can even comprehend. I know it is hard to wrap your mind around going through this for someone else or in answer to someone else's prayer, especially when it is happening to you. But it is. It is so important to understand that if God brings you to it, He has gifted you with the grace to go through it and as you go in retrospect, you will get a glimpse of all the reasons why it was imperative that it was you. Oh, my brother or sister, it is not an indictment of you, neither is it a punishment...it is what the Lord saw in you to make the works of the Father manifest in you. That through your sojourn in the right way, with the right attitude with a heart turned steadfast toward the Lord, the body of Christ would be edified, and the Lord would be glorified.

Look around you as you are going through this journey. What was the prayer of desperation that the person prayed to the Lord that you simply carried out, reflecting God answering them through you? What activation of faith and hope is waiting to be stirred by you as you are at your lowest, most vulnerable time. Who is the Lord bringing to a place that because of the way in which you go through this part of your journey will come to say, Our God... He is God. The Lord really does have the most amazing plan for you.

INTERLUDE

You would think that I would be happy and start jumping for joy right? I don't have to go to treatment every day, the cancer is gone. What is there to be sad about? The truth is a lot. There is a lot that happens at the conclusions of treatment.

While you are happy that the demands of treatment are over, your emotions are all over the place. What is going to happen next? What am I supposed to do without seeing my Oncologist every week, and the team every day? What is recovery going to look like? I have another journey to walk alone in this assignment. When is it going to be over?

There is one who I have identified as a tormenting spirit that is assigned to cancer survivors at this point. He throws thoughts at you like: what if the cancer comes back? Uh! Oh! I don't feel well, is that cancer? Why did I live when so many others have died? ... survivor's guilt is real y'all in a plethora of ways. It's true I am so very fortunate to have survived this, but the guilt that hits me as I see others die, especially vibrant people walking fiercely in their ministries and life assignments, is deep. This is the valley where you wrestle with anxiety and depression because you have to come to terms with the fact that life will never again be "normal" which means the way that it used to be. When they turned me lose from everyday day treatment, I went from seeing the Oncologist every two weeks to once a month, then once a quarter, and finally twice a year. I went from quarterly mammograms to twice a year. I have monthly L-Dex appointments and was given the goal, "If you can make it to 5 years without a recurrence, then your life expectancy will ..." At the 5 year mark I was congratulated. I asked, "What now?" "We really don't know. We haven't had anyone since you've been here, make it this far without a recurrence. Let me call ...." I sat down to listen as I waited. "Well, the plan is for you to make it to 10 years. If you can make it to 10 years, you are no longer a cancer patient but a cancer survivor. Your name won't even be in the registry as a patient anymore, but a survivor." Big deal, I am trying to get to tomorrow.

My body has changed, and I am not talking about 1/3 of my breast being gone. I am talking about the energy and stamina that I used to have. It's gone. I've been told to "prioritize my activity." What does that mean? I live in Lott Land "where we go one, we go all". How am I supposed to choose between going to support one of my children or grandchildren, and going to work? How am I supposed to choose between that revival, and noonday prayer? How am I supposed to choose between cooking dinner, and one of my marathon cleaning, laundry session? What does "prioritize my activity" mean? Take a nap every day? What in the world! I functioned on 4 hours of sleep. I kid you not. I got up at about 7:30 a.m. to be ready to receive the grandbabies. After Mike picked them up from work, I saw patients until 4:30 p.m., I taught at the college from 5 p.m. to10 p.m., and let's not forget while I was watching the babies, I was doing housework and preparing dinner so that my husband could eat when he got home. I would get home at around 10:30 p.m. to11:00 p.m. and study for about an hour or two depending on what the Lord had me digging into at that time. I was the Pastor's wife whose phone was always on and ready to answer for prayer, comfort, and counsel. What do you mean take a nap or at least rest? "Since we know you aren't about to stop." Yet the fatigue was real. I had to adjust in the beginning because cooking a meal wiped me out. Therefore, Mondays and Wednesdays I would watch grandbabies for half a day, then rest, and teach at night. Tuesdays and Thursdays also watch the grandbabies, rest, teach bible study or cook any kind of meal. Friday's was rest day because I was going to be churching like I was crazy and needed all day on Friday to recover. This was new, this was crazy, and this was scary. I had to learn how to NOT carry a purse. They weighed my purse and told me I could only carry what could fit in my pocket. Really? So, to this day I'm like I love purses, but I haven't gone back to them. I don't see the need anymore, hahaha. I have to laugh to keep myself from crying. But other things haven't changed. I am still at that place with God where I never ever want to leave from except to press deeper into Him than I am at this moment. There are things that once seemed so important to me but now are ... insignificant. There are people that I just don't have the energy to deal with and to be honest, I don't understand how I ever did. I am a gym rat because health is in the forefront of my mind. I am focused, I have a purpose .... I have got to make it to 10 years.

Other things have also changed. I spend a lot of time with me. There were lots of Kingdom conversations where the Lord and I took a deep look at Patricia Eileen, and you know what? I didn't like her that much. She survived but didn't live. She had morphed into someone light, years away from the last memory that she had of smiling. I didn't like the fact that she went past passionate to pushy sometimes. She had worried so much about launching her children into their destinies, equipping them to write their stories, that she had ceased writing her own. I didn't like that she was so focused on putting her hand on her husband's back, gently steadying him into what God called him to be, and protecting his feelings. Because until you are a ministry couple in this place, you don't even know ... anyway, that I had allowed the giftedness in me to ... die. I had some long conversations with the Lord just as Saul did that day after the Damascus road experience. He showed me the things that He expected of me for the gospel's sake ... and I liked the end game. We had a conversation not about sin or unrighteousness, but about who He expected me to be as His daughter. It hurt that I was not already there. I didn't like that. I found that from all the talking, I was accused of: A.) Losing my voice, and B.) I had been screaming for years and ... nobody... heard me. But now, I have a new chance. I am starting a new life, and I am about to create and be created into something ... not me. I am ready to start life afresh, new ... but what does that mean? ... What does that look like? It is not so much about getting back to normal as it is finding out what the new normal looks like now. Who has Patricia Eileen become? ... How does she introduce herself to everyone? .... As the caterpillar asks in Alice in Wonderland, the question rings out at this time ..."Who are YOU?"

I also want to take some time in this brief pause to speak to the "domino people". It's been a little while since I just poured out to you, but this is important. Cancer is a long journey. It is not a little hiccup like the doctor said to me on that day. I have found that as people we are only as faithful as the crisis, but we fade away during the long haul.

During that very long 3.5 weeks between diagnosis and surgery, I was falling all over people. "I am here for you." "What do you need?" The list goes on and on. About a week after surgery, life went on. My daughter was back in Atlanta, my brother was back in Virginia, Mike was back working that crazy shift of his, Alex was back to her shift, and hubby was back to work. Jr was the support person, but he also worked half days. Still .... Mom is fighting cancer was still in everybody's mind. There were still the conversations, looks, and tears. Only this time, I was crying, looking, and talking. Then came recovery.

Remember that recovery is a benchmark. Treatment was every day for however long it happens. Recovery was, we are taking away your safety net, your team, your support, and you are going to have to make it without a recurrence for the appointed time. For me, that was 5to10 years. For prostate cancer it is 2 years and so on, and so forth. The same for the death of a child. Everyone is there until about 2 weeks after the funeral, then the person who heard those words is left while life moves on. The same for the person who all of a sudden was without a spouse or job ... life moves on. But the treatment, the funeral, the readjusting is not the end of the road. Your presence and support is needed all the more.

I don't know how it is in your bubble, but in mine, if I am down, I am down. I am pampered and treated like a queen. There is nothing that I need ... or want that doesn't manifest. However, if I get well, mom's back in the game, we can move back to our places. That was so not the case. You know I hated everyone doing things for me because I wanted to do a little something on my own. I guess that's why Miss Abby, and the Big Guy were so important to me during that time. G-Ma could roll on the floor inventing new games like "Floor Tag" and "Tickle me Mikey" G-Ma could be still and quiet, and read us stories and tell us about our history, and about Jesus and that was fine too. It wasn't, "Oh! G-Ma was playing floor tag today, that means she can do this and that and the other, and we don't have to stay in that place of substitution anymore." No, your loved one needs you to understand that it is baby steps for them. Don't smother and keep them invalid, but at the same time, don't rush and thrust them back into the flow of things.

Try to understand that this transition period is exhausting for your loved one. Their life has been forever changed and they are learning what that means, what it looks like, and how it fits them. There are some things that they will never return to. Not because they can't, but because they won't. It is not who they are anymore. Please don't try to force them back into the role. There are some things that they will do that they have never done before. For me it was the development of the "I am going to LIVE until I die" mentality. Please don't stifle or otherwise hinder or try to force them back into that mold. It will only hurt your loved one. Yes, you may be happy and comfortable because they are back to the person that you know and are comfortable with, but it is not okay for them. Your comfort is causing them to be disingenuous with themselves. It is killing them little by little on the inside. You must not be free to be who you are and who you want to be at the expense of your loved one. This will cause resentment to rest behind the smile, the activity, and the relationship. Just take a moment and really, really look into their eyes. Stop your movement long enough to hear what is really in his or her voice.

They have gone through the trenches. They heard those words ... words concerning them ...to their very core. They walked that walk of crisis and treatment. Their lives have been forever changed.

6

TREATMENT WAS EASY... RECOVERY ALMOST KILLED ME

The hand of the Lord was upon me, and carried me out in the spirit of the Lord, and set me down in the midst of the valley, which was full of bones, And caused me to pass by them round about: and, behold, there were very many in the open valley; and, lo, they were very dry. And he said unto me, Son of man, can these bones live? And I answered, O Lord God, thou knowest....Ezekiel 37:1-3

"During the cancer diagnosis and treatment, all the energy and focus is spent on getting through the treatment. Once it's over, the focus switches to establishing "The new normal"--a life that is often much different than it was before cancer." That's what the article said. That... my dear friend, reading this book is an understatement.

You know, for me it **really** hit around year six. The first five years were one mind, one heart, one focus, which was to make it to year five without a recurrence to bring my life expectancy up to 85% of what it would have been before cancer. Yup, I watched my diet. I actually forced myself to eat food and not just live off of smoothies. Well, at least once a day, if I am honest. I watched my stress levels, which was something that I got lectured on every time I saw the doctor during those days. Why? Because stress causes free radicals. Free radicals attached to tissue becomes cancer. My son Mr. Support Person was a watchdog and wouldn't allow anyone to mishandle me. At times I had to say, "Wayne, that was a little harsh wasn't it?" Jr said, "Mom, I was there with you everyday. I saw what you were going through. They are NOT taking you back there on my watch." Michael was walking with me everyday after work. One mile around the walking track while the children played at the playground after he got off work. I like structure so they were singing my song.

I picked up another class per term, but I shut down my practice. It was not a part of my new normal. Something had to go and at that time, between the work of the counselor, treatment planning, and fighting managed care for authorizations with non-psychologists telling me how many sessions I would need to help others get well. I was trying to stay free of a recurrence. I even canceled one of my conference which is something that had never happened once since Shacklebusters was birthed out. I mean, I was focused. I call it my post-op time. But then real recovery hit and living the AD (After Diagnosis) life unfolded, the recovery life hit, and it almost killed me.

What many of you do not realize is that once you hear those words, and you are hurled into that vortex of immediacy, that place where the focus is. It doesn't matter what those words were you now live in the land of, "I have to do this ...to get through this ... to arrive at that." There is not room for anything else except survival. There isn't room for anyone that is going to disrupt or hinder the goal. And then one day you realize all the carnage that lay in your path as a result of this journey. You come face to face with all the situations and emotions that you had tucked into a nice and tidy little place that you could live with while you fought your fight. But now, the chickens have come home to roost and if you are going to move successfully into your new life, you have to deal with the carnage of your old life.

For me, and I have to tread very carefully here because I have been so transparent this entire journey, but I refuse to give up my post as the armorbearer for my husband. I will always sanctify the leader in the eyes of the people. But he is my husband, and this is real. So, I ask of you not to formulate opinions in your mind and heart. Do not conspire with theories that may try to arise. Don't try to figure out what happened. I am not going to put out anything other than what is necessary to make my point about my story. This is my journey, my story, not his.

For me, the hardest part of this was dealing with a broken relationship. When had my best friend on this planet become someone that I loathed and despised? When did it happen that I looked at him and wanted to hurt him? When did I decide that I didn't need him and didn't want him? I had to deal with that. God required it. I could not walk where He was calling me to walk with this red in my ledger. So, I am going to try to unpack this as delicately as I can.

My guy, Wayne the original, I call him. Wow, I have loved him from the moment I laid eyes on him in the fourth grade. I prophesied to my best friend about our life together. It went like this, "Lisa, who is that guy coming out of the lunchroom?" She said, "I don't know. I think he's one of the new kids or a bus kid why?" I told her, "I am going to marry him and have his children before I'm 22" I married him at 18.

Our daughter that didn't make it our Candace was taken from us when I was 22. There was nothing in my life that I couldn't tell him or share with him. He was always the first that I opened up to and spoke with. Now, I could go for days without saying one word to him. Not even, "Would you pass me the ketchup, please". I'd just get up and get it myself. Everything was an argument. Every attempt to talk ended with slammed doors and me in the room crying. What had happened? When had it happened? My guy who was beside me at every major event in my life who I couldn't imagine living without, now I couldn't imagine living with anymore. I Wanted out. To be honest, it was our church that kept me from leaving. Seriously, and they never even knew it. You see, we have a special population of people and they needed to see stability. They needed to see what reconciliation looked like. They needed to see functionality. They needed to feel safe and secure. They are a family of children who would not have survived a divorce and my loyalty to them.... kept me at the foot of the cross and with my husband. What had happened? When did it happen? My guy, who was always my shield and protector, had abandoned me and I didn't like it and I didn't like him? When had Wayne and Patti against the world turn into Wayne and Patti against each other? Why did that happen? Did I even care that it happened? What happened to our family foundational scripture, "Nay in all these things we are more than conquerors through Him that loved us?" Were we even a family anymore? What happened to that? Was it all a lie?

So, let's unpack it the best we can, shall we? I know by now you are asking why was Jr, the support person and not her husband? Well, I asked that too. So did the doctors who, as of my last checkup, I still refused to include him and sent info to Jr. I know because the Lord let me know in one of my repentant kingdom conversations that I needed Jr's crazy out the box faith that matches if not exceeds mine to make it through the journey. But that is not how it felt going through this. My husband was at work. My husband did some very honorable things during my time of struggle that felt like a slap in my face. I am just being honest and had I not been fighting for my life, I would have loved him and applauded him for it. However, these things caused a very deep wound, and we all know what happens to unattended wounds. They get infected and the infection spreads.

He gave some of his leave time to a coworker who was going through cancer so that she wouldn't face financial struggle. That's a good thing, right? But he wasn't using that time to be with me in my struggle. He was at work. That was the doorway that the enemy needed to run through my marriage with a gusto. And that he did. I felt abandoned. I felt as if I came in last place in his life. That his church, his job, his children, his grandchildren all came before me at my most vulnerable time and during the greatest fight of my life.

And so, I totally shut him out of my life. I didn't have time for him since he didn't have time for me. He and all the things that I have lived with, things that I excused as just him, things that perfect love covered, his attitude, his behavior, his thought processes, his action and inaction, his lack of connection. Even in our communication the if I said something and he ignored it, I would have to ask someone I knew he would listen to, to say it to him. If I gave something to him it was never used, but he had no problem with using and wearing something else, his voice, him... he was too stressful for me, and stress causes free radicals and free radicals attached to tissue becomes cancer. I didn't have time for this.

He felt I didn't need him. He was right. I come from good strong stock. I have a lineage of strong women who found themselves having to walk alone and even though in my wildest dreams I never thought that there would be a fight that I had to fight where I would be alone here I was. If I had to fight alone, I was going to fight to win, and I would not fill him in on my struggle. He was no longer worthy of my innermost intimate self.

There was one time I asked him not to go to camp with his cadets because I just wanted him to show some interest in my struggle. It was a particularly hard time in my treatment, and Jane was wearying me. My husband went on with his cadets. I remember sitting in the back room waiting to be called for treatment and he showed up. I was so happy. My heart leapt like it did in the early years when just the sight of him caused my love to gush out and spill over everyone and everything... Wow. In my mind, he had chosen me.

That is, until he opened up his mouth. "Hi" "Hi" "I'm glad I got to see you before you went into treatment" I said, "Yeah, me too. Want to get a burger afterward?" He said, "I can't. One of the cadets got hurt, and I had to bring him into the emergency room" Screech to a halt. Slam on the breaks. You didn't come here to comfort me, to see about me, to be with me. I only see you because you bought a cadet in here. I should have said it. I should have said it, but I stuffed it and it festered and grew inside of me. If I couldn't do it myself and the only alternative was him, it didn't get done. I was hurt beyond hurt and that hurt turned into anger and that anger was on its way to hate.

So, I need to pause the narrative here and talk to those of you who heard those words. This is a pivotal time in your life. I know that it is taking all of your energy to deal with and heal from those words. I know it takes all of your strength and all of your energy. I know it is easier to build a wall and focus on what's here in your face at this present time. But I need to let you know that the enemy of our souls is waiting for such a time as this. The bible says a couple of things about his tactics.

1. He comes in unawares.
2. He comes in while we are sleeping.
3. He comes to steal, kill, and destroy.

Ask the questions. Make the conversation one of the prioritized activities of one of your days. Don't assume, don't make uninformed decisions concerning others, and don't listen to your feelings. Feelings are fleeting and the majority of the time they lie. This is the realm of the enemy. It is the soulish realm (Thank God I don't live there anymore).

If I had asked, I would have found out that my husband attempted to take the time off and his immediate boss, the Major, that I refuse to speak his name, denied it, and blocked it. Does it make me feel better? Not really. I felt then and still feel that he should have fought harder. But then again, that is the soulish realm when, in reality, we had a mortgage and bills, more so since I was not working as much. We had responsibilities and what I call temple taxes with our reformation, and I think wisdom dictates that I say nothing else about that.

So, I don't like his decision and actions, but I understand them. He felt bad about it and could not talk to me about it because I created an environment where, even in my lowest state, I was not safe enough to talk to about it. He had to trust that Jr would pull through. Wow. That changes all the things that the enemy tried to introduce to you about him just now, didn't it? It is hard to admit, but it is the truth.

Another thing that I want to say is that this taught me that my sufficiency was in Christ. I have walked the only me and Jesus walk for real. I have a closeness with him that had this not happened, I would not have been there. I would have been content to have Wayne read the word to me, pray with me, comfort me... keep me. But God wanted to do those things for me. God wanted to be those things to me. Wayne is fallible (I can admit that now) Wayne is human (Since the 1st day he has always been larger than life to me. I told it to Alex like this "Prince Charming fell off of his horse"). But God is not a man. He is all powerful, all seeing, all knowing, and He can do for me what no other can. I no longer want to share God's place and glory with Wayne. It all goes to God. I didn't even realize that I was doing it until it was gone. God will never fall off of His horse, so to speak.

God wanted to change our relationships, both mine and Wayne's and mine and His. He wanted to take me to a new dimension in Him. Me! Can you believe that? It took a minute to wade through all of this... stuff... to realize that me, Patricia Eileen, was worthy enough to go through this alone, not she and Wayne, just God and I to walk it out. He wants the same for you. While I received a God gift from this, the life lessons are invaluable. But if you can, learn from me and don't dig through this on your own.

I want to speak to the domino people. I know you see what is happening. I know that this is confusing for you. I need for you to know that it is time to kick down the wall gently. It is time to snatch your relationships as it were from the fire. It is necessary too fast and pray for the right time, the right tone, and the right heart attitude, but you must act. Your relationships depend on it. Yes, it will be stressful. Yes, it will be unpleasant. But you are worth it. Your loved one is worth it. Did you know that statistically most divorces result from the death of a child, a life-threatening disease, and a loss of identity within the confines of a marriage? It is true. You don't want to be a statistic. The Lord did not create you to be a part of an unnecessary statistic. The Lord came to give life and that more abundantly. Yes, He did. But you have to do your part. If you see the one you love walking toward a wall and a crash is inevitable and imminent you are not going to say, "Well he/she is going through a thing because they heard those words" You are going to act quickly to prevent that devastation from happening. This is what you have to do now. It is the ultimate act of love and understanding.

This is more than likely going to be a book all of its own because there is a reparative work that God wants to do in marriages these days that it is not the point of this book.

Back to this first part of the narrative.

During this time, I also went through a very dark period where I was betrayed by a friend. More on that later. I was fighting for my life, and he would not protect me. (Side note: The Lord told me to be the psychologist to myself that I was to others and all I could hear ringing in my ears were, "Just because Wayne is not doing it the way you want him to doesn't mean that he is not doing it the best he can. How dare you tell him that his good isn't good enough" - OUCH Lord, please stop doing this I want to be angry with him) Even when I had legal advice for him to do a simple thing, he would not do it. There was no justification that he could offer me.

I had to fight that battle alone, and so alone it was going to be. But the Lord said not so. Looking at these and other things while I was trying to live, while I was trying to fight for my life, that had turned into a foreign relationship. One that I didn't know what to do with, who to talk with, who to help me get my head on straight and my heart clean. This was about the worse time of my life. Because I need to be real with you let me say this... Every time I went to God about him, God addressed me. And the more God addressed me, the angrier with him I got. Now he had gone and got me in trouble with God. I will not go further into this. My children and my Sister/cousin know the complete story, but this is not about him.

This is about a broken relationship that happened on my watch because my focus was on getting through the crisis, not on fighting for and working on, or even paying attention to, my marriage. At that time, it was necessary, but now in recovery, it was time to face it. It could not be ignored any more. Things got uncharacteristic between us. The children were having talks with us, and I found myself at the foot of the cross regarding me. Once again, I didn't have time to wait on him and this time it was a good thing. God doesn't care about nothing concerning Wayne when I stand before Him except for my heart, my actions, my thoughts, and my life concerning him. Ouch! That is still a swat from the Father. I needed to get me straight so that I could fight for my relationship. I had to be real before God. In this season my prayer and I am not ashamed to say it here was:

Create in me a clean heart, O God and renew a right spirit within me. Lord, turn my heart back toward my husband and cause me to fall hopelessly and madly in love with him again.

I couldn't pray for anything else. I also confessed all the things I had done or said or felt leading to where we were. Have you seen the movie Sybil with Sally Fields? I felt like her in the end when every time she dealt with a personality, another showed up. I could not stop until I was clean before the Lord absolved of all my unrighteousness in this situation before him. That was the only way to begin to take authority over my relationship to repair, to heal... and then... things got worse. The good news is that I was in a better place. I could fight and I could win and for that I give God the praise.

Let's talk about Job for a minute. The bible tells us that Job was perfect, upright, feared God and eschewed evil. Then he went on assignment, as I call it. And in that assignment, accomplishing the purpose, some things fell out in the wash about Job. Job didn't question God, he did not doubt God; he did not curse God, but he did get put in his place by God. Do you remember that kingdom conversation, "Where were you when I...." Whew, my God today. I had a flashback to a few of my kingdom conversations. See, I had the nerve to feel like this shouldn't have happened to me because I had just gone through something very traumatic to manifest His will here on the earth and really didn't understand.

The truth is that like Job, I was mature in my faith, I was upright in my living, I had a reverential fear of my heavenly Father and well let's put it like this, I have a very real and adversarial understanding with the devil. He hates me and I can't stand him or anything that reflects him, or alerts my Spidey senses when he is a round, that has his tint or flavor. That goes for those who willingly yield their members to him.

Like Job, even though heading into the assignment, the Lord and I had several kingdom conversations. In the recovery stage, like Job, some things fell out in the wash that the Lord had to deal with. There were some things concerning the "after this" that the Lord had to address and to deal with. I think the most prolific message I preached during this period is one that ministered to me but resulted in a 135+ person prayer line was "After this, I'll Live" Taken from Job 42:16. Job lived, and he saw. Excuse me while I praise the Lord, HALLELUJAH! Glory to God. I Love you Jesus and I thank you for the journey. OK, I'm back.

Recovery almost killed me. And again, I am going to be transparent, and I am only going to go so far. When the treatment haze washed away and I was focused on making it to that benchmark, I was betrayed by someone I thought was my friend. This person had spoken some things, and they were not true based on the things splashed out in social media concerning me, my children, and the church.

I can't even begin to say how invested I was in this person because even one sentence will give the identity away. It got nasty. It got to the point that when the lawyer was done, there were 13 felonies committed against me and 9 against my ministry. I was in the cancer registry and as such a protected class. It was bad. These lies and accusations did not consider any of the good that was done, sacrifices made, covering given, just lies. This was a manifestation of "Familiarity Breeds Contempt" I had not let anyone get this close to me in about 20 years and this is the one... that did this to me.

As a result of this, someone who had requested me for a ministry assignment with a monetary deposit demanded a statement from my Pastor to show that these allegations were not true. My attorney said something simple on my social media would suffice. To this day, that has not happened. (and to be honest, today as of this writing and your reading it doesn't even matter anymore) Consequently, this person withdrew his request, and we had to refund the money. Money that had been sown into the next conference so ultimately out of my pocket. Because I did not push for jail time, the ministry fell apart. People accused me of not protecting the thing that God had birthed out of me. They felt that if it didn't matter to me, why should it matter to them. My team of 7 became me and my son. My team, who handled all the business, became me and my other son. It looked as in one fell swoop this thing had attacked and destroyed the very thing that mattered most to me. I understood more than ever Psalm 55:12-14:

"For it was not an enemy that reproached me; then I could have borne it: neither was it he that hated me that did magnify himself against me; then I would have hid myself from him: But it was thou, a man mine equal, my guide, and mine acquaintance. We took sweet counsel together and walked unto the house of God in company."

Anybody else on the planet that had done this thing and I think I would have been able to stomach it. Even if there had been an "I'm sorry, I didn't mean for them to do this or carry it this far" would have sufficed.... This was a terrible thing.

Through this I lost a friend of 35 years. We literally did not talk for about 3 years. When we did it was "Hello" "Hello" "How are you doing?" "Fine. How are you?" "Well, you know" me "Well, I gotta go" her "yeah me too" The Bible says that there is a friend that sticketh closer than a brother and that was her.

Today, you would never know it happened. That is my friend if I never have another friend. It wasn't the first time we fought, and it wasn't the last, but it was the only time that it had been the result of someone outside of the two of us at the causation and it was the only time that it looked as if we would never reconcile. We were tired of the tiptoeing around this thing and the conversation started like this, "You know, there is an elephant in the living room, and it is time to deal with it." She said, "Girl you just get well."

I then replied, "Girl, I ain't bout to act like this ain't there anymore. The Lord is strengthening and sustaining me, and it is time to deal with this baggage and get back to being us." She then said, "I feel the same way this thing between us is killing me and I have just been trying to wait for you to get stronger because I have a feeling it's going to take WORK." I said, "Yeah, to be honest, I have been seeking the Lord as to if there is even going to be an us anymore if this friendship is even worth investing in anymore." She said, "Patti" then silence, her voice was trembling which I had never heard before from her. After about 4 hours we were laughing, and the happy tears were flowing, and we were praying and prophesying, and we are good now.

Concerning that other party, well, the Lord had to heal my heart. Let me put it this way. I had to get to a place where I could give God permission to heal my heart.

You know, one day Father called me to that old familiar meeting place, the top of the stairs and He told me that she never was my friend. I was there for a season and that season was over. The season had been a long season, but it was never meant to be a lifetime thing. The Lord unfolded and opened my eyes to all the red flags, all the things that had been happening all along.

Like the scales were really removed from my eyes. All of the things I just didn't allow myself to absorb. He played back the recording of the things said to my face and outside of my presence. And God is so good that since then I have had it confirmed that the things shown were actually what happened as people are opening up and apologizing for opinions formed and behaviors displayed and conversations that they had taken part in with that person.

He let me know so many times before that I needed to turn her loose and I didn't, so He allowed this to be to free me. To this day, it still hurts for real. I loved her. I love her, but I understand it takes two people to have a friendship, and that friendship takes about as much work, if not more, than a marriage. Someone asked me if she apologizes will all be well.

To be honest, that's in God's hand. As of this writing, I honestly cannot say. I don't know if too much damage has been done if I have just grown away, if the separation was a permanent thing, if I can believe that there is true and sincere admission, accountability, & repentance in anything said or done or even if it is fruitful to do so.

I consider that a desert baby. Desert, baby? I heard a sermon from TD Jakes about desert babies about 34 years ago. The crux of the message was that we all have things we cared about that meant a lot to us, but they were like Ismael, not a part of God's plan for where he is taking you and that like Abraham, we all wander to the edge of the desert and wonder what if... Ah my God... recovery was hard, it almost killed me.

So, if I may speak to those of you who heard those words and now you are sitting in the pool of recovery. I want to take a moment here to say to you, that I hear the Lord saying, "Don't be so quick to call My work the devil. The devil is simply a tool that was used for My will. Regardless of how you feel about a thing, there comes a time when you outgrow that thing. I am not talking about what I have joined together with you." Sometimes we have people who are not capable of going where God is trying to take us, yet are very much capable of being a weight, hinderance, or distraction to the work of the Lord concerning you.

There are those things that were ok, but they are not a part of your new normal and will only contaminate what the Lord is doing in you. Try to remember that old is not new at the same time. Old means used, previously worn, or repurposed. Old is a lot of things but one thing it is not is NEW. If you had your mouth set for a bowl of ice cream and you cracked open the seal and took off the lid and saw not only a scoop out of it but mold around it, no one could convince you that was brand new purchased ice cream. OK, that was gross.

Let me try it this way. There are clothes I had outgrown. Determined to fit them again, I held on to them. Guess what happened when I reached that target size? My taste had changed. I could fit them, but they were uncomfortable for me. The new me was no longer them; they were no longer who I was. I hated to part with them and throwing them out was not an option, but I knew of a ministry that works with battered women and women seeking a fresh start and they hardly ever get plus sized donations, so I called the president and said I had a donation. 3 bags of clothing.

However, there was one outfit that as I went to pack the Lord said, "No" Me being me was like "I don't understand" The Lord said, "Not only does it not fit you anymore but the spirit that it carries is not something that you need to impart to someone else" Gasp! God, please deliver me. (I was still in the place where I felt that everything wrong was me lol). The Lord said, "Not that kind of spirit goofball. You have laid out in that outfit. I anointed you to a high place in that outfit. You ministered in that outfit and even the residual of who you were at that time cannot be haphazardly placed on another. I need for you to seek me, and I will tell you where it is to go." Three days later, I saw the face of someone. Never saw her before, have never seen her since. I had the outfit hanging in my husband's office at the church. It was noon day prayer, and it was me and Jr and I believe one other person.

Anyway, this woman walked in looking for the beauty school next door. The Lord said, "Her!" I walked over to her and told her the school was next door. She said, "You know, the Lord has called me to declare his word and I am so apprehensive..." and I heard my story when I was wearing that outfit come out of her mouth. I said, "Before you go, I'd like to give you something" This woman cried and took me totally off guard by laying down across my feet and praying the blessings of the Lord upon me. She had prayed for a tasteful garment to minister in. The Lord showed it to her and gave her the prayer to pray for the person who gifted it to her." Imagine that.

There was one other outfit the Lord did not allow me to give away, period. He told me to throw it away. He said not only do I not want you to wear it, but I don't want anyone else to be encumbered with it. There was no discussion. I threw it away. By nature of your journey and experience, there are certain things that were ok before you heard those words that can no longer belong to or be a part of you. You cannot go home again, and you should not. Grieve the loss, mourn what you wish could have been, then stand up, square your shoulders, and release it into the desert.

To the domino people reading this, whatever you do, do not try to reconcile what the Lord has separated. Your loved one is in a special place right now. They are on the journey of their new normal. Maybe they have already reached it, maybe not, but one thing is for sure, you do not know the struggle they are going through in recovery. Pray, but don't meddle. If you must inquire to gain understanding, inquire of the Lord. If He deems it your business, He will reveal it, but whatever you do, don't force the new back into the old. It only complicates an already complicated thing.

Moving on.

Another thing that was a very hard pill to swallow that I actually almost walked away from the body of Christ happened not in my church but in my reformation. I will not go into details about this. They are not the message that I want to leave with you. I was approached about presenting something that I was working on. I like, literally had birthed this out and in doing so, it was a part of that publish or perish that doctors face. I had worked on applying for it to become licensed, meaning that eventually it would be used as continuing education credits.

It was this project that I was approached about doing. There was much communication about all the particulars, and I was humbled to do it. I knew that this was the opportunity for many to be activated, so to speak, and that there was a need for it. However, that is not what ended up happening. I had someone reach out to me and say that she had been led by the Lord to come close to me and such. Yet somehow, this person was appointed to handle half of the project. Then it was like insulting because I was told, well I can do the clinical portion and they would do the spiritual part.

So, I am like wait what; I am a licensed preacher of the gospel and a licensed clinician who owned a faith-based practice that kept a waiting list. I should have listened to that voice. It was a trap it was a setup. People had signed up that in all the years I had been going there, I had never seen them. It was electric, and the Lord was moving. But this person was calling me about once every week with changes and directives that I was never receiving myself.

They always came to me under the guise of a friend. I made a statement that things would be easier if they were not changing all the time. This person having the position that they had, took back what I said and whatever else they chose to add to it. Now the diabolical assignment of satan and his plan to kill me shows up.

On the anniversary of my father's death, I was called and, long story short; I was stripped of what I was doing. Seriously! And when I inquired what had happened, what came next was anything but godly. That shook me. I was sitting on the couch crying and asking God to help me make it through the day and this is what happened.

So, after resigning everything that I was doing, I went to my publisher. They got in touch with legal who contacted the reformation. Here we go again. But this was my work. This wasn't their work. There were copyright issues, and I was crushed again. But there was something different about this. I was hurt about a minute; I was confused about five minutes, but I was embarrassed a Philly hour.

Things were said to me that if I am not in the right head space or heart attitude still sting. They hit every insecurity of my youth. They spoke to all of the things that I had overcome in my fight of becoming Patti in the first place. You know, the little girl from Philly who lived on the wrong side of 52nd Street and the wrong side of Market Street. The Patti that was always on the outside longing to be a part and accepted by those who didn't want me as if I was not good enough to breathe the same air as them. Only this time, I didn't have a father or mother to lean on. This time, I didn't have them to speak my heritage and lineage to me and remind me who I am and where I come from.

See in this state, I may not be anything or anybody, but I know that is not the story where I come from and where I have landed but the enemy came and used this to spin me in a way that I still shake my head at. Trust me when a person talks about church hurt... I understand hahaha.

Month after month, I avoided being in that place. Then one of the Administrative Assistant Wives called me and we had bonded, and she pretty much told me I had better be there. I came, and it was horrible. I sat in the back, and she left her seat and came and sat next to me and held my hand throughout the entire setting. She did this for about three months. Yes, seriously.

For the first time since the Lord became my Savior, I went to church out of obligation (pastor's wife and evangelist) not out of a desire to be in His house and among His people. There was no joy, no peace... but then again, there was. The Lord spoke to me and told me, "This is not your city." Something shifted and stirred inside of me. The Lord said, you are needed but you are not wanted. Remember this feeling and only give what I have placed inside of you when I tell you to. I want to direct you, not people. I need you to let your peace return unto you, shake the dust off your feet and watch as I bring you to your tribe."

This was the turning point between beginning and establishment of my new normal and the new me. While being in the right city, I began to hear from the Lord, and I blogged about it. Everyplace you step is not for you. He showed me what the Lord said when sending them to the city. If they accept you, bless them. If they don't let your peace return unto you and shake the dust off of your feet when you leave that city. In other words, that was not your city. I had to learn that just because people gather in an edifice does not mean that gathering is one that I am supposed to be at.

Oh, I have not boycotted it; I am just like wallpaper. I show up; I am invisible, and I leave. But the Lord showed me a company of people that could help to instruct and grow me in what He had called me to in my new normal. People that don't understand your gift will never appreciate it. People who are not focused on what the Lord is growing you in to cannot help you to become. They cannot be your accountability partners nor your covering.

It still saddens and bothers me that not one of those people who had signed up and faithfully attended no longer attends anymore. I learned a valuable lesson or two. One, was there will be times when you are needed but not wanted and my job is to walk away. Another is to make sure that when someone says God told them to come alongside of me to make sure it is a capitol God and not some other god. Another lesson that I learned was that what God births inside of me is not for everybody, no matter how much I want it to be. I am comfortable saying "No."

Finally, I learned that I can actually pray for God to bless those who have despitefully used me. I can completely detach myself from obligation and fellowship. I do not attribute position, assembly, and works for God's place, plan, and presence. When I don't expect things to be what they are not, I am not frustrated and besides, frustration is a spirit that operates through stress and let's see if you remember, stress causes free radicals and free radicals attached to tissue becomes cancer.

Lesson to both those who have heard those words as well as the domino people. This event has changed you, changed the trajectory of your life, forced you to LIVE. You will never be content with or around dead things... things that refuse to change or grow. You don't need to feel bad about the fact that you no longer desire or gain anything of value or substance from them. You can't. It is not who you are anymore. It is not who your loved one is any more. It doesn't mean that there is something wrong or bad, it just isn't for you/him/her anymore and that is Ok. Allow him or her the opportunity to grow and become or he/she will shrivel up and die. Just because you can be there doesn't mean that the one who heard those words can. This is time for a conversation because what is most important is not that the domino people are comfortable but that the one who heard those words can LIVE and not simply exist because it makes others feel good.

OK. Last one.

One day, I was sitting in the middle of the floor, and I still don't know why. As far as I remember, I was rolled over in the birthing position and began to travail. Lord, hee-hee-hee. (Those of you giving birth naturally know exactly what this is) What is this? Lord, "Behold I make all things new" "breath, breath, breath". The Lord took me into an open vision, and I saw the scattered fracture pieces of my ministry and He said to me, "Can I not do you as the potter does to the clay" I said, "Yes Lord" He said, "I want you to stand in the ways, and see, and ask for the old paths, where is the good way, and walk therein, and ye shall find rest for your soul." I replied, "Yes Lord." (tears) He then spoke, "I am about to do a new thing in you concerning Shacklebusters. Speak and release my word over this ministry." I said, "Lord what is your word for this ministry?" He said, "You shall live and not die, and this ministry will be a ministry of deliverance and the yoke shall be destroyed because of the anointing, by fire, and by force."

So, I spake as the Lord had commanded me and I can't tell you how long I had been slain in the Spirit. All I know is that the telephone pulled me out and it was Michael asking if I had gotten his message. That message connected me with a call and that call brought forth a prophecy over the ministry that has shifted Shacklebusters to places I never imagined.

Oh, it doesn't look like it used to, for I am Shacklebusters now, me and the Lord. He has made the ministry again another vessel as seemed right in his hands. Whew! I'm about to run around this room. I can't even get it out. When I tell you that so far, the latter has been greater than the former and it doesn't even look like what it was before it went through what it went through.

This snapshot of the recoveries doesn't even scratch the surface of what lay ahead of me as I transitioned from treatment to recovery and recovery to the new normal. I chose them because they hit four areas that I believe are important for all of those who have heard those words and had their life forever changed. Those four areas are:

1. Things that need to be cultivated, reimagined, and restored in your new normal.

2. Things that need to be released because they are a part of your past. They cannot be allowed to contaminate, stunt you or otherwise keep you in the old, for you will never be that person again.

3. Understanding your new you, your city, and your tribe. Being aware of the need to qualify people you interact with. There is no question of whether you are worthy, needed, and wanted; the question is whether you have been sent, and whether they recognize that. You must determine if they are worthy of what God has designed for you to share with them. When the answer is no, because it will happen, return to your peace, and just keep moving. The Lord sent out the 12, and he told them this very thing. Understanding every opportunity is not your mission. Will help you in the long run.

4. Launching full force into your new normal.

It is my belief that everything that you face as you work through recovery will fall into one of these four categories. Simply put, you are becoming and fine-tuning the result of the struggle. You are now diamonds that have been blown out of the cave by dynamite, chipped away by the pick, and polished into the brilliance that is ready to shine.

I don't want you to think it was all that laborious, for it was not. Taking part in Race for a cure, which will be the next chapter. In rediscovering bowling, and I remembered how much I actually love it. I learned how to laugh for real, the laugh that reaches my eyes. I learned that it is ok to have firm boundaries and that it is OK to not allow others to devalue what God has gifted me with. I think that biggest part for me was learning that it is alright to check the quality of your spirit while in the presence of my atmosphere. What I mean by that is the question is not if I am worthy of your presence in my life, the question is are you worthy enough for me to bring you into my atmosphere.

I accomplished a lot of health goals and learned that I actually enjoy going to the gym. I have become quite the techno girl in that I have learned how to manage my own webpage; I have learned how to do every single thing that others did, which caused me to give bits and pieces of the ministry away. I wrote 7 books and had them published. I tell you I have learned that I have worth and value too. I am 24 karat gold too and even though you may reject me the Lord calls me "HIS" and that's just about the best company that you can ever have.

I have reimagined so many things as the Lord has reordered my living. I dealt with the ugly and I faced my fears as well as my giants and, unlike previously mentioned, I like myself. So, the work of recovery was hard, and it almost killed me. Like giving birth, it took me getting close to death for the Lord to bring new life. Yes, treatment was easy, and recovery almost killed me, but through it all, the Lord made something beautiful out of my life.

7

YOU CAN DO IT

I have fought a good fight, I have finished my course, I have kept the faith:

There were two special gifts that the Lord gave me through this journey that I struggled in choosing which one to end this letter to you, my fellow sojourner. One was the night I walked the red carpet with the Imagine Me Foundation's Celebration of Life for Cancer Patients and Survivors. While I have no words for that experience, I find it would only be valuable for those who heard those specific words ... "Cancer" so I have chosen to not talk about that here.

I am choosing to leave this journey with the Race for a Cure. My race for a cure. I told you in a previous chapter that I started planning my 1-year cancer free party before surgery. I shared that nothing about that journey was normal or ordinary, and one of the victories that I shared was the race for a cure. I think I was like 5 months into treatment. Remember, it was a double dose because of God's favor. I worked and never missed a class the whole time, so the class was a special kind of class. I had two classes that bonded on a very personal level and to this day we keep in contact and there is simply a lasting bond and love shared that transcends academia. One was when my father was in the process of dying and one was going through cancer treatment.

One night, a student announced that she was going to race for a cure. She asked if I had someone that I wanted to walk for me. She was going to do Team Lott because I was so fiercely fighting cancer and she wanted to do this for me. I said, "Yeah. Me," I talked to my doctor about it, and he was like, "No. You are not strong enough," I was like, "I don't remember asking your permission, I thought I was just telling you that I was going to do it." "I just don't think you are ready" "I'm doing it" I told the children what I was going to do. All of them offered to wear my number and walk for me. "Nope," I said, "I'm walking my own race" "I'm walking with you," each of them said. Little Bit came up from Georgia for it too. The surprise was on her as she had cut her hair to be in solidarity with me, but I never lost my hair.

Every day, Michael walked with me until I was up to three and a half miles. I was determined to get to five. I trained. I rested. I was determined. I will never forget that day as long as I live and even as I type, the tears are flowing down my face. Team Lott was so much more than me and my three. My husband wanted to come, but it was sacrament Sunday, and He was the Pastor, and his two elders were walking with me so he couldn't come. Alex wanted to come, but she had a baby and a two-year-old, so she stayed and supported my husband because she understood wanting to be there and not being able to.

Please don't take this the wrong way, but I believe it had to be this way. I won't get into my miracle birth stories here, but this moment in time it was just me and my children. It was like it was scripted long before I even knew it and...well...it was... wasn't it? Something about this was... I just don't have the words for it. We pulled up, and I went to sign in and there was my class, not one, not two, it was my class. I looked and there was my oncologist, my L-Dex Dr, and my anesthesiologist (remember him). The Doctor said, "If you are determined to do this thing,

I figured that I better be here in case you need medical attention. I have a picture with each of my children by the wall pointing at my number and they each wore my number because if at any time I needed to stop, they were going to finish my race for me.

And so, we began to walk. Every few blocks, one of my children was, "Mom, you okay? You need to rest? You need to take the cart back? I'm here to walk for you" "Nope, I'm good" Every couple of blocks, "Hey Doc, you looking good. You are doing good Doc. Keep up the good work Doc" And so it went. The minutes turned to hours, and I was doing fine, but in my body I was slowing down. My breathing got harder and Mr. Support person aka Wayne Jr, barks out, "Slow it down, Mom. That's it, I'm walking for you" Little Bit is, "Un-un June (Jr), take her back, I got this" but Mike, my (oh I wish I could call him my personal nickname for him here) my Mike was "Mom, remember the active park. You got this!" Ah dissention in the ranks. I can do this lol. But I did slow it down. We stopped more often, and I made it a point to stay hydrated and catch my breath more often.

At that last stop for water, we were told that we were almost done just a quarter of a mile to go. Then it happened. I turned the corner and there was the biggest hill I had ever seen, with the steepest slant that I had ever seen, and all the wind left me.

I knew at that moment that I couldn't do it. I had made it this far, but I wouldn't finish my race. I stopped with my head down and my hands on my knees in total defeat and surrender, and the children were right there. So were three of the students. I hugged Little Bit in tears and said, "I can't do it." I looked over her shoulder and saw my Doctor nodding yes.

Something happened, those children refused to walk for me. Every few blocks, they were saying that they would walk for me, but now that I needed them to do it, they wouldn't. One of my students turned backward and started walking up the hill backward right in my face. When I went to look around her, one of the other students was on her right, the other to the left. I couldn't see anything ahead of me but these three soldiers who were my students. (literally, and thank you for your service to me and our country) Jr linked up in my right arm, Michael in my left and Little Bit put her hand on my back. (I can feel them as I write at this moment it is so etched in my being).

My student Paula says, "Doctor Lott, you got all day, you don't have to rush you don't have to hurry, just once step at a time." I say, "I can't" Little Bit says, "We got you Mom" The boys tightened their grip and so we walked. I would take about three steps and stop. "Doctor Lott, you got all day, you don't have to rush, you don't have to hurry, just once step at a time." "We got you Mom" for what seemed an eternity but was really only half an hour this continued and then, the cheers, the whistles, the claps, and the hugs. Team Lott was there waiting, and I had crossed the finish line. I was awarded a medal and the tears wouldn't stop.

I had fought a good fight; I had finished my course; I had kept the faith. This was symbolic of my journey and of the journey that you are on whatever journey that may be, whatever words that you have heard, whatever the assignment that you are walking out. It is in you. You can make it.

You feel alone and, in a very real sense, you are alone. Alone in that you heard those words. However, as alone as you are, you are not alone. You have a community. You have support and encouragement coming from places that you never expected. You will have days when it is a breeze, and you will have days when there has to be someone in your face reminding you that you don't have to be on anybody's timeline but your own. You have all day, so to speak.

Just take your time and keep moving. You have people looking out for you and when your strength is gone and you feel as if you just can't make it anymore, there will be your domino people showing up on each side with their hand in your back steadying you and giving you strength reminding you that "You Got This!"

I don't know what the words were that you heard, but what I do know is that it knocked you for a loop. They changed not only the trajectory of your life, but they changed you. I don't know the length of your journey neither do I know all of the obstacles that you are going to face but what I do know is that if you have gone into covenant with God about it and He has cause this to be your current assignment or situation; He has gifted you with the grace to complete it.

You are so very special to God. Just think, He chose you for this. He saw the opportunity for His work to be made manifested in the earth through you and all of the chaos and turmoil that those words caused. Yes, He did. It is messy; it is challenging, and you are never going to be the same, but He is with you, and He has strengthened and empowered you for the job or He wouldn't have given it to you. I don't know where you are on your journey, but I know that God's Got YOU. Simply KEEP THE FAITH!

EPILOGUE

EPILOGUE

I would like to start this off with a poem that has had meaning to me since I was 16 years old, but never as much as through my darkest moments of recovery. I pray that it blesses you as it did me, or at least pulls things back into perspective for you. It is titled "The Tapestry" and it was written by Corrie Ten Boom.

*My life is but a weaving between my God and me. I cannot choose the colors
He weaveth steadily
Oft' times He weaveth sorrow; And I in foolish pride Forget He sees the upper
And I the underside
Not 'til the loom is silent and the shuttles cease to fly Will God unroll the
canvas and reveal the reason why
The dark threads are as needful in the weaver's skillful hand As the threads of
gold and silver In the pattern He has planned
He knows, He loves, He cares; Nothing about this truth can dim. He gives the
very best to those Who leave the choice to Him.*

I never thought that I would be in this place. But I am so glad that I am. I am writing to you because I hate loose ends and in my AD (After Diagnosis) life, that is something that I never do.

Since the end of our journey, the Lord has been good to me. In 2019, Wayne and I celebrated 41 years of marriage!!!!! I know, it was awesome!!! He texted me in the middle of Bible Study and said, "Pack your bags, we're going to Hawaii" and three days later we were on our way. It was wonderful. Such a special week. Such a special anniversary. The stuff dreams are made of.

In 2020 we like everyone in the world were sheltered in place as the coronavirus ravaged the land. I will always treasure that time and not because My Guy gutted my kitchen and built me a kitchen that I can't describe either. It was a blessing because we were together. I got to see the insanity of his job. I have to tell you I would have quit a long time ago but then again, the charge to cover and keep was given to him and he is doing a great job. I was in the house with him and there were days that went into nights that I wondered what in the world is wrong with these people. Yet we found a way to make it.

One of my favorite things about being married to Wayne is that we get to go minister together. That was something that I feared had died. However, more than doing ministry with Wayne, I love being the woman that God created me to be in this hour. I am doing things that I never imagined that I would do. I am "fearlessly fierce", and I love it. I have a totally different outlook and refuse to ever, ever go back to my BC (Before Cancer) self.

Who would have imagined that I would be the host of a weekly television show in 7 different countries. Me! Look, I thought Facebook live and YouTube live were daunting, but now every Friday I link on to the patch and allow the Lord to do what He has said. He told me to name it Speak to My Heart because there are those who need someone to cut through all the fluff and foolish and get back to touching the heart of the people.

And true to His word that I would walk in deliverance, each week I am getting emails and messages of people being delivered in one way or another. The guests that I am directed to bring on are always nervous because the only thing that I ask them to do is to put their ear to the Lord's mouth and their emotions to His heart and speak to the heart of the people. It is amazing. When I was told that I was going to the nations I didn't quite picture it like this, but then again as you travel with me you know that my "Yes Lord, You can use me" didn't quite look like I thought it would either.

I also have a weekly broadcast called Foundation Training. It started as a virtual bible study the thing that I love the most about it is that the majority of the regulars are not from my church... or any church. They are not super saints; they are the ones who had walked away from the church because of the behavior of those in the church. These are people seeking a Savior who makes a real difference in the hearts and lives of people. Then there is the daily devotional that the Lord has me writing for this same group of people.

There is Wednesday Word and Flash Ministry that the Lord has placed upon me when he wants to release a word over the people. I am very busy for the Lord. Me, the "little girl from Philly who lived on the wrong side of 52nd Street and the wrong side of Market Street."

I did not resume my practice, though I kept my license current. I believe that the Lord wants me free to minister to the people in a way the office restricts, and the current policy of the land doesn't permit. A total surprise to myself is that I decided to start a travel business. Who would have thought? God knew. On this side of the journey, what I didn't have room for was what I was in. There is very little that remains from what was. And I really do like myself. I have journals upon journals of kingdom conversations as well as prophetic words from the Lord and in the words of my church mother, "If she say it, look for it to come with a quickness" hahahahaaaa. Oh, there is so much that I want to share with you in catching you up.

The Lord has instructed me in this season to not only remember the why, but to cause his children, the ones who have guardianship over the precious body of Christ, to remember the why. Remember why the Lord Jesus came in the first place Remember what it is that we are called to do. Remember what the mission of the church is supposed to be. To let them know that He is not pleased with the strange fire at the altar, nor the strange gods that have taken His place. He is disappointed in those priests who have abandoned their post for the spoils and admiration of this world. He has told me to remove the complications of Salvation and live a holy and separated life. And that is just about the most fun that I have in my BC (BEFORE CANCER) life.

However, the main thing that I wanted to share was this. YOU were a part of this assignment. I know in the book I talk about the seven people that this cancer was purposed for, but I was mistaken. I have come to realize that there were 8 manifestations that the Lord wanted to do and that 8th one is you. Eight is representative of new beginnings, and that is exactly where you are and where I was at the end of the book.

Hearing those words, believe it or not, it is the first of your new beginnings. Treatment and recovery is the second of your new beginning. Your New normal is your third and final new beginning. Just like King David received three anointings, so have you. I didn't understand as I was living this and even in the midst of it why the unction to write was so heavy upon me. I knew it was more than simply journaling, but there was always something that kept pushing me that the assignment would not be complete until the story was told.

You, my brother, and sister, who heard those words. The purpose of this was to shift your narrative and help you realize you don't need to feel bad about anything, and you didn't do anything wrong, and yes, this is a gift from God as crazy as it seems. You, the domino, people needed this. You needed to understand that the Lord had called your loved ones to something that you will never understand and because they have changed, if you press in and walk alongside of them you will be changed as well. Change is what was needed. Change is good. Especially when it brings us into alignment with the will and Word of God.

There is one final fight that I have that I need to share with you. That is the fight to stay in the place that you walk in right now. Going through this journey after the yes and the covenant, there is a place that you go in God. I mean, no amount of fasting can get you there. There isn't enough money to get you there. You can't meet the right people and people's appointment can't get you there. This is a place that comes from total surrender and dependence on God. This is a place where he is just as present with you as this book that you are reading. It is a place where, at times it is as if you can reach out and touch him. It's a place where His glory, abides. It is a place where you don't just get glimpses of an opened heaven, but you are granted entry to the presence of God in his atmosphere and not Him come down into yours. Oh, it is a magnificent place.

The thing is that as time goes on and you heal as you return to or embrace your new normal, there is a fight to stay in that place. This is a place of sacrifice, and only you can determine if you are done with your assignment. You are content to LIVE life, or if you are determined to stay in this place in the presence of God. For me, it was simple. I never ever ever want to, not EXPERIENCE God like this. Even if it means that my relationship with Wayne has to change. No matter if that means I don't take what I have just anywhere, because someone told me so. Even if it means there are times that I know you are upset and disappointed with my choices and my ministrations. Trust me, I am equally disappointed that you have not chosen to get to truly know God in the fellowship of his suffering. That you have chosen carnality and pseudo spirituality over holiness and righteousness. So, it is a struggle. And you will struggle as well. However, Jesus makes the difference, and He is more than worth it.

So now I have met you, and I have shared with you, and I have felt you. I have felt you in every page of this book. I have felt you in every story shared, every tear shed, every prayer prayed. I had to write this just for you. Oh, I know that this is not for everyone, this is for you, and I pray the Lord continues to strengthen and sustain you as you travel the path leading to your new normal. I pray for blessings of peace and joy and energy and that your faith fails not. If you need me... just holla. I will pick you up in my spirit and pray. If you need to talk, reach out. I'll be there.

From the Heart,

Patricia Eileen

Dr. Patricia Lott is a retired Marriage and Family Therapist and an Adjunct professor at a local university. She is also the author of the New Book No More Again Forever, Marcie Mouse series , Shhh We Don't Talk About That, Shacklebusting Scripture Studies, and the Lady Lott Prayer Clinic Series.

Married to the love of her life Pastor Wayne Lott Sr. closest to her heart is that of being a mother to Wayne Jr., Michael (Alexandria), Elisabeth-Grace and grandmother to Abigail-Eunice and Michael Jr.

In her spare time, you can find her talking with people on the streets, feeding the hungry in the area and clothing the homeless. She never tires of letting people from all walks of life know that they have worth and value.

Connect with Dr. Patti at:
https://www.drpatricialott.com
http://www.shacklebusters.org/

MY SUPPORT TEAM
(DOMINO'S)

My Guy and I in Hawaii

Race For A Cure

From Treatment to The Retreat

No More Again Forever Message

CPSIA information can be obtained
at www.ICGtesting.com
Printed in the USA
BVHW090732181021
619189BV00016B/463

9 781087 982496